The PERCY LETTERS

Correspondence of PERCY & PATON

THE PERCY LETTERS

DAVID NICHOL SMITH &
CLEANTH BROOKS, *General Editors*

The CORRESPONDENCE
of THOMAS PERCY &
GEORGE PATON

Edited by A. F. FALCONER

New Haven

YALE UNIVERSITY PRESS

1961

60322

Introduction

I

After the second edition of the *Reliques* had appeared in 1767, Percy decided to collect material for a third and larger edition and also to prepare another publication under the title "Ancient English and Scottish Poems, chiefly of the more popular cast, accompanied with some few modern pieces." [1] It was in this way that his correspondence with George Paton began, and their letters make it possible to follow the fortunes of both projects.

Early in the correspondence, Percy explains that he is anxious to recover "all sorts of ancient Poetry whether Printed or Manuscript, particularly those fine old Scottish Songs and Ballads which are so much admired for their simplicity and artless unaffected beauties." [2] His view is that "it is nearly as much merit to retrieve them from that oblivion which they are falling into, as to compose them at first." [3] Paton, in his turn, sends ballads, songs, notes, illustrations, "scarce things," and Percy, with good reason, speaks of "innumerable obligations."

From 1768, Percy worked at intervals on his "New distinct Independent Publication" [4] and on a fourth volume for the *Reliques*. He was allowed to borrow the Bannatyne Manuscript from the Advocates' Library to assist him, and he transcribed "a great Part of the Contents" of the Maitland Manuscript,[5] but when a third edition of the *Reliques* was published in 1775, the intended fourth volume was not added. It had not been given up, for he assures Paton: "I hope now in the Course of next Winter to prepare a 4ᵗʰ Volume of Reliques for the Press." [6]

[1] *The Correspondence of Thomas Percy and Sir David Dalrymple, Lord Hailes,* ed. A. F. Falconer, Baton Rouge, 1954, pp. xv–xvi.

[2] See Letter I, p. 1.

[3] See Letter V, p. 13.

[4] See Percy-Hailes *Correspondence,* p. 122.

[5] See Letter CVI, p. 158.

[6] See Letter LXXXIII, p. 122.

But there were delays and, in 1778, when Percy was made Dean of Carlisle, he realized that he could "hardly find a Vacancy now from more serious persuits." [7] Paton readily agreed that the claims of the Church or, as he puts it, "the superior and more interesting concerns of Mankind" [8] must come first.

Percy then had hopes that the publication of his "large fund of Materials" might be undertaken later by his son,[9] but the youth died at Marseilles in 1783. Three years before that, a considerable part of his collection of ballads, songs, and romances had perished in an outbreak of fire at Northumberland House, London.[10]

The fourth volume of the *Reliques* and the "Ancient English and Scottish Poems" did not appear. Circumstances, and not any lessening of Percy's interest, had decided their fate.

Yet it would be easy to make too much of this, and to see it as a more serious loss than it is. The *Reliques* as they stood had had an influence that, of its kind, was without precedent, and what had been achieved by the three existing volumes was greater than anything that could have come of merely adding to their number. Others took over where Percy left off, and much that he had in mind, indeed much more, became the work of Ritson, Ellis, and Scott.

II

Though the greater part of the correspondence with Paton consists of requests for manuscripts, ballads, rare books, and antiquarian information, it reflects more than the particular interests of a scholar and an antiquary. It is yet another record of that enthusiasm for the past that was part of the history of the age. Much in it, too, shows the way being prepared for the emergence of Sir Walter Scott and discloses the background to his wide achievement in ballad, song, and lay; romance, tale, and novel; history, biography, and antiquarian research. For in all these, Scott was the heir of the eighteenth century.

References to historical works or sources keep recurring, and it is interesting to note that if arranged in order of date they show how the writing of Scottish history grew and developed. There is a pro-

---

[7] See Letter CVIII, p. 162.
[8] See Letter CIX, p. 163.
[9] See Letter CVIII, p. 162.
[10] 5 April 1780.

gression from heroic poem and rhymed chronicle, represented by Barbour's *Brus* and Andrew of Wyntoun's *Chronicle*, through prose histories in Latin and Scots, by Fordun, Boece, Major, Dempster, and Lindsay of Pitscottie, with the contributory studies of archivists, numismatists, and antiquaries, right on to the work of Hume and Robertson. And finally, a new development is seen in the *Annals of Scotland*, where Sir David Dalrymple, Lord Hailes, employs a scientific method that anticipates the nineteenth and twentieth centuries.

Revived interest in earlier Scottish literature led inevitably to the compiling of glossaries. Much had been done in England from the time of Speght's *Chaucer* (1598), but in Scotland there was nothing of note before Ruddiman's glossary to Gawain Douglas's *Æneis* (1710), which laid a foundation for later work. Glossaries were added to Allan Ramsay's *Ever Green* (1724), Lord Hailes's *Ancient Scottish Poems* (1770), and David Herd's *Ancient and Modern Scottish Songs* (1776); and, as the *Reliques* contained an important selection of Scots ballads and songs, Percy, too, found it necessary to include Scots words and phrases in his glossaries. In this, he was helped by Lord Hailes and his friends and later by Paton: ". . . let me know what words are not so intelligible and I shall furnish you an Explanation afterwards." [11] But explaining words by correspondence is a slow way of working, and it came to be felt generally that plans for a comprehensive Scottish dictionary ought to be made. Johnson commended the task to Boswell in 1769, saying, ". . . you will do a useful thing towards the history of the language." [12] Paton was anxious to see a beginning made: "both learned and unlearned can offer a mite here," [13] and his letters to Percy and others reveal some preliminary steps that were taken.

The first definite proposals came from Dr. William Cuming of Dorchester,[14] who wrote to Paton that he had "long earnestly wish'd for the publication of a Dictionary of the Scots Language," [15] and

---

[11] See Letter III, p. 9.

[12] 19 October: see *Life of Johnson*, ed. G. B. Hill and L. F. Powell, 1934, II, 92.

[13] See Letter XCI, p. 133.

[14] See Letter XCI, n. 3, p. 133.

[15] 27 March 1776 (National Library of Scotland, Adv. MS. 29-5-8, Vol. II, ff. 44–46).

suggested that a society should be formed to produce it. Throughout 1776, he kept urging his scheme: "I chearfully give my Suffrage for electing the ingenious and respectable Ld. Hailes as President of the Society." [16] He also tried to interest Richard Gough,[17] who replied that he was in sympathy [18] and made this known to Paton.[19] In the interval, Paton had taken the matter up with Percy.[20] Realizing that a dictionary would be "a labour of much time and application" which could not be "confined to the industrious Collection of one Person," Paton proposed that, to start with, the glossaries in the *Reliques* might be rearranged and extended and so prepare the way for the main scheme. Though this was not done, the method he suggested was actually followed long afterwards by Lord Hailes, when drawing up a collection of Scottish proverbs in 1791, and is briefly described in one of his letters giving directions to Paton: "I have made a sketch of a Glossary. Of this I have cast off a very few copies: I send you two and beg the emendations and additions of yourself and friends." [21]

It was not until the appearance of Jamieson's *Etymological Dictionary of the Scottish Language* in 1808 that these early hopes were fulfilled. Paton was among those who subscribed to it, but he did not live to see it published.

III

George Paton

"I was comfortably amused with Mr Paton, who was formerly a Bookseller, is Grandson to Mosman the printer, and has a great knowledge of Antiquities and curious Books."—Boswell.[22]

[16] 6 July 1776 (*Ibid.*, f. 47; also 14 September and 19 December 1776, ff. 48–49).

[17] 22 May 1776 (Bodleian Library, MS. Gen. Top. C.8. No. 25525, ff. 403–04).

[18] 26 May 1776 (*Ibid.*, f. 404).

[19] 30 May 1776 (Gough-Paton MSS., National Library of Scotland, Adv. MS. 29-5-6, Vol. I, f. 64).

[20] See Letter XCI, p. 133.

[21] 6 April 1791 (National Library of Scotland, Adv. MS. 29-5-8, Vol. I, f. 47).

[22] *Private Papers of James Boswell from Malahide Castle*, ed. Geoffrey Scott and Frederick A. Pottle, 18 vols., New York, 1928–34, Vol. XII, p. 182.

It was this knowledge of antiquities and rare books that gave Paton
a place in the literary society of Edinburgh during its most brilliant
period, and that led to his correspondence with a wide and distinguished circle.

Though his executors considered that he had "contributed more to
the aid of the Antiquary and Topographist than any man of his
time," [23] it does not seem to have occurred to any of his friends to
write his biography, and the few sketches attempted after his death
by those who had no acquaintance with him are scant and unsatis-
factory.[24] There is, however, enough information in his unpublished
correspondence and in records at Edinburgh to make it possible to give
an outline of his life.

"My Forefathers," he tells Gough,[25] "resided in The Parishes of
Muckhart and Dollar for the Space of nearly four Centuries and
were Vassals of the Argyle Family for that Period, the former of
which parishes were once inhabited only by the Name or Clan of
Paton, altho' no Record or written Monument can be adduced for
this Fact, every such Testimony &c having been destr[o]yed by
the Marqus of Montrose during the Grand Rebellion last Century
when both parishes were laid in ashes, for the private difference between these two noble Families, who according to the Humour
of the Times ravaged each their possessions to the utter loss of the
poor Inhabitants. No evidence of establishing this Fact remains at this
Time but the rural Monuments at their Graves as their Names or
Initial Letters; at this time there are few of that Surname who reside

[23] *Catalogue of the Remainder of
that Very Interesting Collection made
by the late Mr. George Paton . . . ,*
Edinburgh, 1811, Prefatory Note
(National Library of Scotland, MS.
T.2.d.i).

[24] James Maidment, *Letters from
Joseph Ritson, Esq. to Mr. George
Paton,* Edinburgh, 1829, 8°, Prefatory Notice. *A Series of Original Portraits . . . by the late John Kay,*
Edinburgh, 1837–39, 2 vols., I, 244–
47. Sir Daniel Wilson, *Memorials of*

Edinburgh in the Olden Time, Edin-
burgh, 1848, 2 vols., I, 163–64.
Thomas Constable, *Archibald Consta-
ble and his Literary Correspondents,*
Edinburgh, 1873, 3 vols., I, 20–21,
397–98. Hans Hecht, *Songs from
David Herd's Manuscripts . . . ,*
Edinburgh, 1904, pp. 3–8. T.F.
Henderson, *Dictionary of National
Biography.*

[25] 25 June 1787 (National Library
of Scotland, Adv. MS. 29-5-7, Vol.
II, n.f.).

there and no Tombs worthy notice do remain but one of Bishop Paton [26] who was inhumed there a Great &ca Granfather of mine he was B. of Dunkeld in James VI reign. . . ."

Born in Edinburgh on 23 June 1721,[27] George Paton was the fifth of the family of four sons and four daughters [28] of John Paton [29] and Margaret Mosman.[30] His father was a burgess of some standing, a bookseller, one of the founders of the Royal Infirmary, a member of the Revolution Club,[31] and, for a time, bookbinder and bookseller to the University of St. Andrews.[32]

Though it is invariably stated [33] that he remained all his life a bachelor, Paton married [34] Rosina,[35] daughter of James Paton, minister of Carrington, or Primrose,[36] in 1762. She died ten years later.

Among his notable relatives were James Gillespie (1722–91), Principal of St. Mary's College, St. Andrews: "my old Schoolfellow and Relation"; [37] Thomas Craigie [38] (d. 1751), professor of Hebrew at St. Andrews and, in 1746, successor to Francis Hutcheson in the chair of Moral Philosophy at Glasgow; and Robert Oliphant of Rossie (1718–95), Postmaster General for Scotland.[39]

[26] James Paton of Middle Ballilisk (c. 1520–96), created Bishop of Dunkeld in 1572.

[27] Edinburgh Register of Baptisms, H.M. Register House, Edinburgh.

[28] Two sons and two daughters did not survive childhood. The others are Margaret, born 1715; William (1720–1807), minister of Eckford, Presbytery of Jedburgh; Anne, born 1722. Paton speaks of the death of an only sister in 1789. It is not known whether this was Margaret or Anne. See n. 42 *infra* and p. xiii.

[29] d. 1766.

[30] 1683–1771, daughter of George Mosman, bookseller in Edinburgh.

[31] "List of the Members of the Revolution Club" (Edinburgh University Library, MS. Dc. 8.37).

[32] St. Andrews University Library (MS. Z 325 S3 P2).

[33] *Dictionary of National Biogra-* *phy,* following earlier accounts. See n. 24 *supra.*

[34] 21 February, *Edinburgh Marriage Register, 1751–1800* (Scottish Record Society).

[35] 1717–72. He mentions her death to Gough, 1 September 1772 (National Library of Scotland, Adv. MS. 29-5-7, Vol. I, n.f.).

[36] In the Presbytery of Dalkeith. In 1703 the name Carrington was changed to Primrose but has been resumed.

[37] To Gough, 30 January 1788; also a letter to Professor William Barron of St. Andrews, 8 December 1791 (Edinburgh University, Laing MSS., II, 453, f. 2).

[38] To Gough, 29 November 1774. He was succeeded at Glasgow by Adam Smith.

[39] 1718–1795. To Gough, 21 August 1786.

Apart from mentioning that he went to school at Perth,[40] Paton throws no light on his school days. He may have attended the Grammar School there, but the records do not confirm that he was a pupil. Whether he spent any time at school in Edinburgh, it is not possible to determine from the evidence.

In early youth, he entered the bookseller's business which his father had inherited from his father-in-law, George Mosman. There, in "that Shop high and laigh, back and fore lying on the north side of the Parliament Closs within the Town of Edinburgh,"[41] he began to acquire his great knowledge of books and to form the remarkable library that brought him so many friends and correspondents. But the inheritance was not free from legal entanglements, which gave rise to recurrent lawsuits over a period of thirty years and led to the failure of the business in 1760.[42]

Paton had to seek another means of livelihood. He was not without influential friends, and they may have helped him to secure the post of clerk in the Customhouse, where, for almost half a century, his days were spent in exacting office work. Hours were long and there were few breaks. "I wearie much for a very few days' Amusement," he tells Percy, "but must pospone it till some time hence."[43] As he grew older, longer hours were enforced, and this, he admits to Gough, "is exhausting to me at my time of Life."[44] His friends deplored that he was misplaced and that his gifts were misapplied. "What Pity it is that a Man of his Erudition and endowed with such an ardent Zeal for promoting the Knowledge of the Antiquities of this Island should be confined to a Desk and summing through the several Variations of the four Rules in Arithmetic!"[45]

He was overworked and underpaid. From 1767, his salary remained fixed at £60 a year,[46] and his friends, who speak of this sum

[40] To Gough, 21 February 1792.
[41] Register of Decreets (Dur. Office), Vol. 409, H.M. Register House, Edinburgh.
[42] This has been investigated by Mr. R.P. Doig in an unpublished thesis, "George Paton: a Study of his Life and Correspondence" (St. Andrews University Library, MS. Z 1004. P2 D7, pp. 23–29).
[43] See Letter LXXIV, p. 110.
[44] To Gough, 14 March 1791.
[45] Cuming to Gough, 7 February, 1784 (Bodleian Library, MS. Gen. Top. C.8. No. 25525, f. 540).
[46] Customhouse Accounts, H.M. Register House, Edinburgh.

with a sense of outrage, met with no success in their attempts to have it increased.[47]

Financial setbacks seemed part of Paton's lot. He mentions them sometimes to Gough, not to invite sympathy, but, characteristically, to explain why he is not buying more books: "I have met with some considerable Losses of late that I will restrain the Passion of picking up the County Descriptions for some Time: till Stocks recruit." [48] Or, ten years later: ". . . it has long been my desire to make a purchase of the whole Set of your Antiquarian Engravings which are to be sold, but have been so often shifted by a Writer (or an Attorney as you term them) here, that I cannot get a Sum from him which has been long in his hands these many years, and am affraid will loss the whole, this is disagreeable." [49] But if he denied himself, he was always ready to help any venture that would further literary, historical, topographical or antiquarian studies. Only a few weeks before, he had written to Gough about a proposal of Thomas Pennant's for publishing George Low's journal of a tour through Orkney and Shetland: ". . . which I wish with all my heart as this completes the whole Survey of Scotland: . . . if you approve of this Scheme and think this would take in London, I would be very happy that Mr Low made a small mite by it as he lost some time ago any small pittance he had collected: for my part tho' I've lately suffer'd in a similar degree by the insolvency of some, yet will chearfully contribute my small mite (as I formerly promised) of five Guineas to promote the publication." [50]

He was easily imposed on, and occasionally gives a brief sketch of those who have deceived him. He finds himself unable to come to the aid of his relative Ben Waters, having, as he says, "been misfortunate enough some time past to lose some money that I did not expect by a pretended friend, with whom this gay supercilious world

---

[47] See *Archibald Constable and his Literary Correspondents*, I, 397–98. Chalmers to Paton, 6 March 1800 (National Library of Scotland, Adv. MS. 29-5-8, Vol. IV, f. 121); Gough to Paton, 24 March 1800 (Adv. MS. 29-5-6, Vol. II, f. 106).
[48] 1 May 1772.
[49] 8 November 1783.
[50] 24 September 1783.

at the present day does too much abound." [51] There were, too, books borrowed and not returned, and coins "pocketed by inspectors." [52] But the worst of these misfortunes came in his seventy-third year, when a large part of his savings was swept away in the failure of the banking firm of Bertram Gardner and Company.[53]

The changing years brought hardship and grief. The death of his "affectionate, amiable only Sister" [54] in 1789 left his household desolate; "A Loss to me irreparable—this Calamity has been very grievous to me and will require a very long period 'ere I can recover my Spirits to attend properly to be able to answer my worthy Friends Letters." [55]

Of the little attention given to Paton's life this last phase has had most. But it is misleading to fasten on it as some have done,[56] and to leave an impression that Paton was a recluse and ascetic. This is not what his letters or portraits [57] suggest, nor what his friends say of him. Most of his days had been passed in a companionable and hospitable family circle, and his way of living became austere only when this was broken.

Even in those difficult years he kept adding to his library, and it was partly from concern for his books that he "engaged in a new private toil of moving to another house," [58] twice within a year; first from Liberton's Wynd [59] to Forrester's Wynd [60] in 1790 and then, in 1791, to the house in Lady Stair's Close [61] with which he has come to be exclusively associated.

When he reached the age of eighty, his official duties were much lightened and may have become nominal.[62]

[51] To Ben Waters, 1 February 1786 (National Library of Scotland, MS. 3648, f. 136). See n. 73 *infra*.

[52] To Gough, 24 April 1795.

[53] To Gough, 25 August 1794.

[54] To Gough, 7 November 1789.

[55] To Gough, 25 November 1789.

[56] See n. 24 *supra*.

[57] There is an etching by John Brown (1752–87) in the National Portrait Gallery, Edinburgh, and one by John Kay engraved in *A Series of Original Portraits*, I, 243.

[58] To Gough, 14 March 1791.

[59] To Gough, 24 July 1790.

[60] Williamson's *Directory for the City of Edinburgh*, 1790–92.

[61] Aitchison's *Edinburgh Directory*, 1793–94.

[62] The cash books of the Customs show that, from 1801, a deputy was acting for him and it seems reasonable to infer from the entries that Paton received at least half of his full salary. The matter is examined by Mr. R. P. Doig, *op. cit.*, pp. 23–29.

He died on 6 March 1807 in his eighty-seventh year, and was buried in the churchyard of Greyfriars.

His valuable library was sold by auction in 1809, and the remainder of his collection, consisting chiefly of manuscripts, maps, drawings, prints, and coins, in 1811.[63]

"You attend to your friends at all times," John Davidson of Haltree fittingly said of him,[64] and the Earl of Buchan showed his regard by assuring him: "If ever you should find yourself disposed to retire from the smoak and bustle of Edinburgh, come to Dryburgh Abbey, and I will give you a cloyster in my garden." [65]

Paton's sincerity is seen not only in his friendships but in his conscientious, scrupulous ways: "Please know that Fordoun cost nothing so no more can be charged for it." [66] Casualness in scholarly matters annoyed him. A lawyer from Lorne had been careless in correcting proof sheets for Gough, and Paton reports: "took the opportunity of reading to him the paragraphs of your last reflecting on his and others overlooking in the triffling manner the Sheets, which so nearly concerned their place of Nativity, I then took occasion to smartly chide him for his treatment." [67] Good-natured though he was, he could resent discourtesy. He had helped to found the Society of Antiquaries, but later observes to Gough: "being not so well treated as expected so have no further connection with them." [68]

Much sound sense and discernment appear in his critical judgments. In the controversy over Chatterton, he saw clearly that "his Genius had great merit" and that "with riper compositions he might

---

[63] The catalogue, with prices marked, is preserved in the National Library of Scotland (T.2.d.1). The sum realized for the library was £1355.6.11.

[64] 15 September 1788 (National Library of Scotland, Adv. MS. 29-5-8, Vol. IV, f. 35).

[65] David Steuart Erskine, eleventh Earl of Buchan (1742–1829), National Library of Scotland, Adv. MS. 29-5-8, Vol. III, f. 63; also *Letters* *from Thomas Percy, D.D. Afterwards Bishop of Dromore, John Callander of Craigforth, Esq. David Herd, and Others, to George Paton* [ed. James Maidment], Edinburgh, 1830, p. 176.

[66] See Letter LXXII, p. 107.

[67] To Gough, 9 August 1787, referring to Mr. Peter MacVicar, writer.

[68] To Gough, 2 December 1800. Paton held office as a curator.

have truely deserved the uncontroverted esteem of poetical ad-
mirers." [69]

In politics, Paton inherited Hanoverian sympathies. He was no
Jacobite. The victory of Prince Charles Edward at Prestonpans was,
in his view, an "unhappy Catastrophe," [70] and his dread of any
challenge to settled government led him, in the American War of In-
dependence, to take sides with George III and his ministers. John
Witherspoon, President of Princeton College, was for him "this
Trumpeter of Rebellion" and Congress "that rebellious Cabal." [71]

He does not seem to have thought of keeping any family correspondence. Though his brother, the clergyman at Eckford, wrote
to him frequently,[72] there is no trace of their letters. But a few from
Paton to his relative Ben Waters [73] have survived, and the good
humor and interest in day to day things shown in them make it re-
grettable that so little is known of this side of his letter writing:
". . . wish you had sent more particularly how large or small your
hatt ought to have been as I may not so justly get you fitted in that,
however hope you shall appear as spruce as any of their Frenchified
Gentry." [74]

With scholarly correspondence, it was different. Paton was as
careful in preserving the inquiries and communications of the men of
letters, antiquaries, lawyers, topographers, and naturalists who sought
his aid as he was unsparing in his efforts to serve them. He had over
seventy correspondents. With some only a few letters were ex-
changed, but his correspondence with Gough runs to more than
seven hundred, and though this is by far the largest, a considerable
number passed between him and Pennant, George Low, Lord Hailes,
George Chalmers, the Earl of Buchan, David Herd, William Thomson of Oxford, William Cuming of Dorchester, John Davidson,
and Thomas Percy.

---

[69] See Letter CIV, p. 155.
[70] See Letter IV, p. 11.
[71] See Letter XCIX, pp. 145–46.
[72] This can be gathered from Paton's correspondence with Ben Waters.

[73] Benjamin Waters (*fl.* 1811), merchant and seaman at Wick and, from 1788, at Leith.
[74] National Library of Scotland MS. 3648, f. 125.

Paton's handwriting is copper-plate in character and very regular, but regularity is not a mark of his style. His main concern is to pass on information, and he sets his thoughts down as fast as they come to him with breaks, asides, and repetitions, and does not trouble much with syntax. Plain idiom, with echoes of everyday speech, is blended quaintly with literary and official phrase. But his style has vitality and, in its individual way, reflects his personality and the setting of his life, conveying something of the "attentive hurry" of the Customhouse official and the "studious pleasure to serve" of the zealous antiquary.

". . . so leave that Article to your own choice and mode of expressing it as I chuse only to point out the real facts. . . ."[75]

IV

The Manuscripts

The extant correspondence of Percy and Paton is now published completely for the first time.

Most of Paton's letters to Percy are preserved in the British Museum (Add. MS. 32332), five are in Harvard University Library (bMSS Eng 893, 124B-D, 9E, and 124G), and two in the Bodleian Library (MS. Percy, C.1, ff. 60–65). Add. MS. 32332 also contains a letter from Paton to Robert Lambe, a letter from John McGowan to Percy,[76] a letter from Paton to Hugh Blair and one from Blair to Paton, a receipt by Percy for the Bannatyne MS., two letters to Percy from Alexander Brown, Librarian to the Faculty of Advocates, a letter from John Wotherspoon to Paton and one from Wotherspoon to Percy. All these, except the letter from McGowan to Percy, are printed in this volume.[77]

Percy's letters to Paton are in the National Library of Scotland (Adv. MS. 29–5–8, Vol. I, ff. 51–94). Thirty-six were published

[75] To Gough, 17 June 1779.
[76] Printed in Percy-Hailes Correspondence, Appendix I, p. 157.
[77] Extracts from a few of the letters were included in Hans Hecht's Songs from David Herd's Manuscripts (Edinburgh, 1904) and in The Bannatyne Manuscript, edited by W. Tod Ritchie (Scottish Text Society), Edinburgh, 1934, 4 vols., Vol. I.

in James Maidment's *Letters from Thomas Percy, D.D. . . . David Herd, and Others to George Paton,* Edinburgh, 1830.

A note in Paton's hand, evidently intended for Percy, is among the Anderson papers in the National Library of Scotland (MS. 1001, f. 61).

To Professor D. Nichol Smith for his deep interest in this volume and his advice at all stages of its preparation, it is a particular pleasure to express thanks.

To Professor Cleanth Brooks for many services and for seeing the volume through the press grateful acknowledgment is made.

Acknowledgments are also made to Dr. William Beattie, Librarian of the National Library of Scotland, Mr. William Park, Keeper of Manuscripts, Mr. D. M. Lloyd, Keeper of Printed Books; by Mr. G. H. Bushnell, Librarian of the University of St. Andrews, Mr. Dugald MacArthur, Sub-Librarian, and Mr. R. G. Cant, Dr. R. H. Carnie, and Dr. R. P. Doig.

Permission to use manuscripts in their possession was kindly granted by the Trustees of the National Library of Scotland, the British Museum, the Bodleian Library, Yale University Library, Harvard University Library, the Museum of the Rosenbach Foundation, and by the Faculty of Advocates, Edinburgh.

A. F. Falconer

St. Andrews
June 1960

Editorial Note

Simple contractions of common words have been expanded when there can be no question of the full spelling: but contractions of which the expanded form is not certain, and all titles, such as L^{d} for Lord, are given as they are in the manuscript. Parentheses have been substituted for square brackets so that brackets may be reserved for interpolations by the editor.

Table of Letters

I

From Percy[1]

Northumberland House, London
April 30. 1768.

Sir,

Mr Lamb[2] of Norham (who has been very obliging in collecting literary Curiosities for me) has communicated to me the Contents of a Letter[3] you were so good as to write to him: wherein you very genteely offer to favour me with the sight of any curious poems in your possession; as also to assist me in collecting anything of that sort in your power. This Offer is very obliging, and too agreeable for me not to accept of it. You desire me to inform you what sort of pieces I am desirous of collecting.—I answer all sorts of ancient Poetry whether Printed or Manuscript, particularly those fine[4] old Scottish Songs and Ballads[5] which are so much admired for their simplicity and artless unaffected beauties: Historical | Ballads, would, [p. 2.] in a more particular manner be exceedingly acceptable.—Dr Blair[6] will (at my request which I have made him by this Post) lend you three Volumes of Ancient Songs and Ballads[7] lately published in London, which will shew you, better than I can describe by Letter, what sort of things I am principally fond of; tho' any good old

[1] *Source:* National Library of Scotland, MS. 29-5-8, Vol. I, f. 54; printed in *Letters from Thomas Percy . . . to George Paton*, ed. Maidment (hereafter cited as Maidment) p. 1.

[2] Robert Lambe (1712–95), of St. John's College, Cambridge, vicar of Norham from 1747 to 1795. See James Raine, *The History and Antiquities of North Durham*, 1852, p. 264; *Alumni Cantabrigienses; Letters of Joseph Ritson*, ed. Harris Nicolas, 1833, 2 vols., II, 228; *D.N.B.*

[3] See Appendix I, p. 167.

[4] Over "beautiful" deleted.

[5] Percy had included twenty Scottish songs and ballads in the second edition of his *Reliques of Ancient English Poetry*, 1767.

[6] Hugh Blair (1718–1800), critic and divine and, from 1762, Regius Professor of Rhetoric and Belles Lettres in the University of Edinburgh.

[7] The second edition of the *Reliques*. A copy with many corrections in Percy's hand is preserved in the Museum of the Rosenbach Foundation in Philadelphia.

Poetry will be acceptable, provided I have it not already. I shall now inform you what I am already possessed of. viz.

1. Gawin Douglas's Virgil [8] folio.
2. Old Blind Harry's Poem of Wm Wallace.[9] 4to
3. The Old Poem concerning Robt Bruce.[10] 4to
4. Sir David Lindsay's Poems. (a bad edition.[11] 12°)
5. The Evergreen. a Collection in two Vol^s 12mo [12]
6. Drummond of Hawthornden's Works.[13] folio.
7. Allan Ramsey's Tea-table Miscellany.[14]
8. The Charmer 2 Vol^s of Songs. &c.[15]
9. Many little Poems printed at Glasgow, as The Battle of Harlaw,[16] Hardyknute,[17] &c.

[8] *Virgil's Æneis, Translated into Scottish Verse, By The Famous Gawin Douglas Bishop of Dunkeld,* ed. Thomas Ruddiman, Edinburgh, 1710, folio.

[9] *The Acts and Deeds of the Most Famous and Valiant Champion Sir William Wallace . . . , Written by Blind Harry in the year 1361,* Edinburgh, 1758, 4°. See Letter III, p. 7.

[10] *The Life and Acts of the Most Victorious Conqueror Robert Bruce, King of Scotland. By John Barbour, Archdeacon of Aberdeen,* Edinburgh, 1758, 4°. See Letter II, p. 4.

[11] Unidentified.

[12] *The Ever Green, Being a Collection of Scots Poems, Wrote by the Ingenious before 1600,* Edinburgh, 1724, 2 vols., edited mainly from the Bannatyne MS., by Allan Ramsay. Both this and the second edition (1761) are in small 8°, not 12°.

[13] *The Works of William Drummond of Hawthornden,* ed. Bishop John Sage and Thomas Ruddiman, Edinburgh, 1711, folio.

[14] *The Tea-Table Miscellany or a Collection of Scots Songs.* There were four volumes. A copy of Volume I dated 1724, believed to represent the first edition and to be unique, is preserved in the Huntington Library. But the Sterling Memorial Library at Yale possesses a copy, printed from a different setting of type, dated 1723. Copies of Volumes II and III dated 1726 and 1727 were found in the library of the Earl of Haddington at Mellerstain, Scotland. Burns Martin conjectures that Volume IV was published in 1737. See his *Allan Ramsay,* Cambridge, Mass., 1931, pp. 97–98.

[15] *The Charmer: A Choice Collection of Songs, Scots and English,* Edinburgh, 1749, 12°; 1751–52, 2 vols., 12°; 1765, 1 vol., 12°.

[16] The earliest printed version extant is that in *The Ever Green,* 1724. But see the note in F. J. Child's *The English and Scottish Popular Ballads,* Cambridge, Mass., 1882–98, 5 vols., Part V, p. 316.

[17] *Hardyknute, a Fragment. Edinburgh, Printed by James Watson,*

I should be very glad to borrow the *Collection of Scots Poems* [p. 3.] *printed by Andro Hart,*[18] which you mention, or anything else of the kind described by me above. It may be left with Dr Blair (Professor of Belles Lettres in your University) who will in a few Days take a Journey to London,[19] and convey anything to me, that you will please to send. A letter by the post may be directed to the Revd Mr Percy, and inclosed under Cover To his Grace the Duke of Northumberland, at Northumberland House London.

I am, Sir,

Your Most obliged

Humble Servant

Thomas Percy

II

From Paton[1]

[May 9, 1768]

Sir

I received yours of 30th past and am obliged to Mr Lamb for informing you of my Answer to his Letter about two months ago.

Printer to the King's Most Excellent Majesty. MDCCXIX. Folio, 12 pages. The Bodleian Library has an undated octavo edition (entered in the Catalogue as "*c.* 1720"). Printer's ornaments show that it came from the same printing-house as the 1719 folio. *Hardyknute* was included in *The Ever Green,* 1724, II, 247–64, and reprinted by itself with notes in London, 1740, 4° (Dodsley), and in Glasgow, 1745 and 1748, small 4° (Foulis).

[18] *Ane Compendious Booke of Godly and Spirituall Songs,* Edinburgh, printed by Andro Hart, 1621, 8°. See an account of earlier editions in *A Compendious Book of Godly and Spiritual Songs,* ed. A. F. Mitchell, Edinburgh (Scottish Text Society), 1897. See also Letter II, p. 4, Letter III, p. 6, and Appendix I, p. 167.

[19] Percy's Journal (British Museum, Add. MS. 32336–37) for 23 May 1768 reads: "Today Dr Blair and Lord Alg^n Percy arrived from Scotland before Dinner. . . ."

[1] *Source:* British Museum, Add. MS. 32332, f. 13.

I have the first Edition of *The Reliques of Ancient Poetry 3 Vol. 12°,* but long'd much to see the Printer do more Justice to your Labours,[2] it will yield me Pleasure if I can promote your further Intentions and shall be ready to contribute as far as in my Power.

It has not yet been my good Fortune to meet D[r] Blair, how soon the present attention to the office Business permits I shall wait of him and, ere he set out put into his Hands the few Things by me with what else either printed or manuscript I can collect, and what of the latter may ocurr, You may depend on my occasionally transmitting them in Course of Post.

I am obliged to your giving me the Catalogue of what Scot's Authors you have already, which if you please to increase in London, by looking into *Allan Ramsay's Poems* [3] *2 Vol. 12mo* reprinted some Years ago there, as also *W. Thomson's Orpheus Caledonius* [4] *2 Vol. 8° Lond. 1733.* If you cannot easily meet with the last Book, which is now scarce, you may command the Use of it from me, it containing many of our old Scots Ballads and the very best Copies; in Ramsay's Poems are many old Scottish Poems revived by him, which are of a much more antique date than his day, but of this more particularly after you have perused the Book.

What I design to lend you by Doctor Blair are viz.

1. The Collection of Poems printed by Andro Hart (exceeding rare) 12°.
2. Watson's Collection of Scot's Poems [5] Vol. 1st in 3 parts 8°. N.B. no more was ever printed of it.
3. Gordon's History of R. Bruce [6] 12°

[2] Printer's errors occur mostly in the prose dissertations. There are few in the ballads.

[3] *Poems by Allan Ramsay,* 1761, 8°, 2 vols. Earlier *London* editions were 1751, 8°; 1733, 12°; 1731, 8°; Edinburgh edition, 1721–28, 4°, 2 vols.

[4] William Thomson, *Orpheus Caledonius,* 1725, folio, 1 vol., and 1733, 8°, 2 vols. Of Thomson little is known; he was alive in 1763: see Percy-Hailes *Correspondence,* p. 21, n. 16.

[5] *A Choice Collection of Comic and Serious Scots Poems . . . ,* issued in three parts, Edinburgh, 1706, 1709, 1711, 8°, printed by James Watson.

[6] *The Famous Historie of the renown'd and valiant Prince Robert, surnamed the Bruce, King of Scotland . . . by Patrick Gordon,* Dort,

4. Sir David Lindsay's Works [7] 12°. This is the best Edition I've seen tho' will not boast of it's correctness, or perfection but it may be usefull to compare with your Copy.

There are some Old Ballads and Songs in Manuscript promised me, which shall have a place with the above.

You may depend on hearing from me in a few Posts when I will give you a further List of our Scot's Poets, but if you please to consult D[r] George M[c]kenzie's Lives of the Scot's Writers [8] 3 Vol. fol. you may find many there mentioned which may excite your Curiosity. I must observe the Hon[ble] M[r] Walpole [8] has used him much in his Royal and Noble Authors tho' the Printer all along has named him Sir George M[c]kenzie, instead of D[r] George M[c]kenzie.

I shall apply to several Acquaintances to make | Search in their [p. 2.] Liberaries for Your Use, which if obtained will make me happy, and shall be communicated to you.

I hope to hear from You soon and am

Sir

Your most obedient Serv[t]

GPaton

Custom house Edinburgh
   9 May 1768

1615; reprinted Edinburgh, 1718, 12°; Glasgow, 1753, 8°.

[7] Paton sent the Edinburgh edition of 1648 (see Letter III). *The Workes of the Famous and worthie Knight, S[r] David Lindsay . . . , Edinburgh, Printed by Gedeon Lithgow Anno Dom., 1648*, 8°.

[8] George Mackenzie, M.D. (1669–1725), *The Lives and Characters of the most Eminent Writers of the Scots Nation*, Edinburgh, 1708–22, 3 vols., folio. Horace Walpole's error occurs in his *Catalogue of the Royal and Noble Authors of England*, second edition, 1759, 8°, II, 201–10.

III

From Paton[1]

[May 13, 1768]

Sir

Since writing you this Week I have seen Doctor Blair, who informs me that he sets out on Tuesday first with whom you may expect a Loan of the following Books viz^{lt}

1. Collection of Godly &c^a Sangs printed by Andro Hart
2. d^o of Comic and Serious Scot's Poems 3 parts in one volume printed by James Watson 1713
3. Sir David Lindsay's Works Edin^r 1648
4. Gordon's History of Robert the Bruce Edin^r 1718

I shall be extremely glad they can be of any Service to you, with which you will likewise receive

1. Specimen of a Book intituled Ane Compendious Book of Godly and Spiritual Sangs [2] &c^a printed by Andro Hart.
2. The Chearfull Compainion [3]
3. Ajax's Speech [4] &c^a

which if you think worthy to be placed amongst your Collection it will give me pleasure.

---

[1] *Source:* British Museum, Add. MS. 32332, f. 14.

[2] *A Specimen of a Book, Intituled, Ane Compendious Booke, of Godly and Spiritual Sangs* . . . , Edinburgh, 1765, 8° in fours, edited by Sir David Dalrymple, Lord Hailes. *Cf.* title, Letter I, n. 18, p. 3. Percy already had a copy. See Letter V, p. 13, and Percy-Hailes *Correspondence*, p. 109.

[3] *The Chearful Companion: A Collection of Songs,* Edinburgh, 1766, 12°.

[4] *Ajax his speech to the Grecian Knabbs . . . attempted in broad Buchans,* by Robert Forbes, Aberdeen, 1742, 8°; Edinburgh, 1754, 8°; Glasgow, 1755, 12°.

You will let me know whether you have seen or desire to have any of the following Books or Pamphlets and I will send them up to you afterwards. vizt

1. Harvey's Life Robert the Bruce a Poem ^{5} 4°
2. Samuel Colvill's Mock Poem or Whig's Supplication ^{6} 12° in [p. 2.] Scot's Hudibrastic
3. Captn Montgomery's Poems ^{7} 8°
4. Edom of Gordon ^{8} a Scottish Poem 4°
5. Gill Morice ^{9} d°   4to
6. Young Waters ^{10} d°   4to
7. The Thistle and the Rose ^{11} &c^a 8°
8. Hamilton's Life of Sir Wm Wallace ^{12} 8°

---

^{5} John Harvey (*fl.* 1726), *The Life of Robert Bruce King of Scots. A Poem*, Edinburgh, 1729, 4°. It was reprinted without the author's name as *The Bruciad, an epic poem in six books*, 1769, 8°.

^{6} Samuel Colvil (b. 1616?) of St. Salvator's College, St. Andrews), matriculated 1631/32, M.A., 1634, wrote *The Whiggs Supplication or the Scotch Hudibras. A Mock Poem, in two parts*. The author's MS. is in the Bodleian Library (MS. Eng. poet. e. 48). It appeared in Edinburgh, 1657, 8°; London, 1681, 8°; Edinburgh, 1687, 8°; 1695–1710, 12°; London, 1710, 12°; St. Andrews, 1796, 12°. Colvil also wrote *The Grand Impostor Discovered*, Edinburgh, 1673, 4°. See a note on the author in *The Scots Peerage*, ed. Sir James Balfour Paul, Edinburgh, 1904–14, II, 550. (The *D.N.B.*, 1887, and the *Concise D.N.B.* confuse him with his elder brother Alexander.)

^{7} Alexander Montgomerie (1556?–98). (The "buryall of Alex^r Montgomerie poet" is mentioned in the MS. records of the Presbytery of Edin-

burgh, 22 August 1598.) *The Poetical Works of Captain Alexander Montgomery*, printed by Robert Urie, Glasgow, 1754, 8° in fours.

^{8} *Edom of Gordon; an ancient Scottish Poem. Never before printed. Glasgow: printed and sold by Robert and Andrew Foulis M.DCC.LV.*, small 4°, 12 pages. See *Reliques*, 1765, I, 99–106.

^{9} *Gill Morice, an ancient Scottish Poem. Glasgow, Printed And Sold by Robert And Andrew Foulis. M.DCC.-LV.*, small 4°, 15 pages. See *Reliques*, 1765, III, 93.

^{10} *Young Waters, an ancient Scottish Poem. Never before printed. Glasgow, printed and sold by Robert and Andrew Foulis M.DCC.LV.*, small 4°, 8 pages. See *Reliques*, 1765, II, 172.

^{11} *The Thistle and the Rose*, Foulis Press, Glasgow, 1750, 8°.

^{12} William Hamilton of Gilbertfield (*c.* 1665–1751), *The Life and Heroick Actions of Sir William Wallace*, Glasgow, 1722, 8°, an abridged and modernized version of Blind Harry's *Wallace*.

I have not pick't out (from a Manuscript Catalogue by me) a List of some Scot's Poets, but will do it soon and write you if any of them are to be met with here, and if possible endeavour to procure you a Loan of them.

You will observe at the End of these Poems printed by Andro' Hart is "*Quod King James the First*": some here do not think that King James wrote these Poems, alledging them to be of a much later Date; vizt about the Time of the Reformation, and seem to attribute them to the Promoters of it from a Passage in a M.SS. History of the Church of Scotland written by Mr Rowe [13] Minister of Perth in K Charles II Reign where he says "*The Reformation in Scotland was much forwarded by Sir David Lindsay's Poems and Satyrs, with Poems by Mr Wedderburn*" [14] *&c* but of the last I can

---

[13] Paton has confused persons and dates. The history was written by John Row (1568/69–1646), minister at Carnock in Fife. He received some of it *viva voce* from his father, John Row (1526–80), the reformer, minister at Perth, and from papers left by his father-in-law, David Ferguson (1560–98), minister at Dunfermline. His son, John Row (*c.* 1598–1672), rector of Perth Grammar School and later Principal of King's College, Aberdeen, made additions to his father's work. There were several MS. copies in circulation and the printed versions show variation in their use of these sources. The work was first published as *The Historie of the Kirk of Scotland*, M.D.LVIII.—M.DC.XXXVII. *By John Row, Minister at Carnock. With Additions and Illustrations By His Sons*, edited by William Fleming, Maitland Club, Edinburgh, 1842. Another edition appeared in the same year: *The History of the Kirk of Scotland, From the Year 1558 to August 1637. By John Row, Minister of Carnock: With a Continuation to July 1639 by his Son, John Row Principal of King's College, Aberdeen*, edited by David Laing, Wodrow Society, Edinburgh, November 1842.

Paton's quotation differs verbatim but not in substance from both the printed versions. See Maitland Club edition, p. 3: "But the more particular meanes quhairby came the knowledge of God's trueth in the tyme of great darknes, were such as Sir David Lindesaye's Poesies, etc., Wedderburne's Psalmes, and Godlie Ballads of godlie purposes, ..." Cf. Wodrow Society edition, p. 6: ". . . such as Sir David Lindesay his poesie upon the Foure Monarchies, . . . Wedderburn's Psalmes, and Godlie Ballads, changeing many of the old Popish Songs unto godlie purposes. . . ."

[14] See Letter XXXII, p. 42. The greater part of the "Gude and Godlie Ballatis" (See Letter I, n. 18, p. 3.) is traditionally ascribed to the brothers Wedderburn, James (*c.* 1495–1553); John (*c.* 1500–56); Robert (*c.* 1510–57).

find no Account. I do rather believe these Sangs &c^a are K. James I [15]
as he contracted an Aversion to the Romish Clergy and fancied
Wicklef's Principles during his stay in England, however this is
submitted to your own Opinion.

Inclosed you will receive the "Lasses Lamentation for the Loss of [p. 3.]
their Lovers slain at the Battle of Flowden," [16] a Young Gentleman
told me he transmitted to Mr Dodesly the *"Jews Daughter"* [17] which
was design'd for your Use.

How soon I obtain from some of my Acquaintances any manuscript old songs &c I will transmit them in Course. I presume this
requires no Glossary but if it does let me know what words are not
so intelligible and I shall furnish you an Explanation afterwards. I am

Sir

Your most obedient Humble Ser^t

GPaton

Customhouse Edinburgh
  13 May 1768

[*From Paton to Dr. Blair* [18]]

George Paton presents Compliments to Dr Blair
sends the following Books vizt

1. Compendious Booke of Godly and Spiritual Songs by K. James I
   printed by Andro Hart.
2. Sir David Lindsay's Works
3. Gordon's History of Robert the Bruce

---

[15] James I, King of Scots (1394–1437).

[16] Probably "The Flowers of the Forest," by Jean Elliot (1727–1805), third daughter of Sir Gilbert Elliot, second Baronet of Minto. It was circulated anonymously in Edinburgh in 1756.

[17] "The Jew's Daughter" had already appeared in *Reliques*, 1765 and 1767. Paton's copy contained some variants (see F. J. Child's *English and Scottish Popular Ballads*, ed. Helen Child Sargent and George Lyman Kittredge, Boston and New York, 1904, p. 370), but they were not adopted in *Reliques*, 1775 or 1794.

[18] *Source:* British Museum, Add. MS. 32332, f. 15.

4. Collection of Poems printed by J. Watson
5. A Specimen of a Book &ᶜ reprinted by Lᵈ Hails
6. Curious Collection of Scot's Poems 1767 [19]
7. Chearfull Companion.

which Dʳ Blair will please give to the Reverᵈ Mʳ Percy at London, to whom he wrote last Night that the above were put into Dʳ Blair's Hands.

Customhouse Edinburgh 14 May 1768

  Address: To The Revᵈ Dʳ Blair
    with a Parcel

IV

From Paton[1]

[May 27, 1768]

Sir

Having been much confin'd with the Business here it has not been in my Power to compare the Second Edition of the Reliques of Ancient Poetry with the first, which I have by me: but hope to do it soon, this is a Pleasure for me to enjoy.

This day was put into my Hands "Sir James the Ross" [2] which is

[19] *A Curious Collection of Scots Poems,* Edinburgh, 1767. It includes "Ajax his speech. . . ." (See n. 4 *supra.*)

[1] *Source:* British Museum, Add. MS. 32332, f. 18.

[2] "Sir James the Ross, A Historical Ballad," by Michael Bruce (1746–67). It appeared in the posthumous volume *Poems on Several Occasions. By Michael Bruce,* Edinburgh, 1770,

12°, pp. 30–42, and is based on the story of the ballad "Sir James the Rose." (See Child's *English and Scottish Popular Ballads,* ed. Sargent and Kittredge, p. 503.) It was printed frequently in chapbook form. It is included in the Appendix to Lambe's edition of the *Battle of Flodden,* Berwick on Tweed and London, 1774, 8°, p. 118, and in the notes, p. 100, is ascribed to "Miss Christian

inclosed, it is most abominably printed but could find no better, after all the Search I made, the Occasion of it I am utterly a Stranger to, but will make further Inquiry and if it merit your Attention shall communicate what I can learn of it.

You will likewise find another Ballad on the Battle of Preston composed by an East Lothian Farmer Mr Skirving [3] tho' modern, yet is absolutely the most just Discription of that unhappy Catastrophe [4] we had, it was written some few Days after it happned.

I hope you have got the few Things from Dr Blair. whenever any thing offers afterwards shall be sent you.

I am

Sir

Your most humble Servt

GPaton

Customhouse Edinburgh
   27 May 1768

V

From Percy [1]

London, Jun. 12. 1768

Sir,

I received the very kind favour of your Letter, and the packet of Books you were so good as to send me by the hands of my friend

---

Edwards, daughter of a gentleman in Stirlingshire, author also of several other poetical pieces."

[3] Adam Skirving (1719–1803), farmer in East Lothian and writer of songs, the best known being "Johnnie Cope." Paton refers to the "Battle of Tranent Muir," which celebrates the rout of the government forces by Prince Charles Edward at Prestonpans in 1745.

[4] Paton clearly had no Jacobite sympathies.

[1] *Source:* National Library of Scotland, MS. 29-5-8, Vol. I, ff. 52–53; printed in Maidment, pp. 5–9, where it is misdated 12 *January 1769.*

Dr Blair; I ought to have thanked you for these obliging Civilities
more early, but trusted to your Candour for indulgence and deferred doing it till Dr Blair's return.—By the D^r I have returned
such of the Books as you were so good as to lend me: viz.

    1. Collection of Godly &c.Sangs. by Andro Hart.
      (This is very curious indeed, but I cannot believe it earlier than
      the Reformation; Certainly not K. James Ist's.)
    2. James Watson's Collection &c.
      (This I have in my own Collection.)
    3. Sir David Lindsay's Works.
      (This is a fine Edition much better than mine)
    4. Gordon's Hist. of Robt Bruce

[p. 2.]   For the other pieces which you are so good as to present to me, I
beg you will accept my kind Acknowledgments. I have nothing
equally curious to return at present, but hope you will accept a little
piece which I lately printed for the use of my Parishioners intitled
a Key to the New Testament.[2]—

    Should I print any more Volumes [3] of Ancient Poetry, you may
certainly depend both upon a Copy of the Book, and of my acknowledgments in the Preface for the obliging Assistance you are so good
as to afford me, both in picking up scarce things for my perusal, and
in favouring me with such Illustrations as occur to you.—The *Battle
of Flowden* [4] is a fine pathetic Elegy: Dr Robertson [5] had favoured
[p. 3.] me with a Copy of it before.—*The Jew's Daughter,* (which you | say
was transmitted to Mr Dodsley by a friend of yours for my Use,
never reached me, and Mr Dodsley says he knows nothing of it:) I

[2] *A Key to the New Testament,*
1766; second edition, 1773. Though
modestly intended by Percy for his
parishioners, it came to be used at
Oxford and Cambridge. It was frequently reprinted.

[3] Percy at this time intended to do
so. See Percy-Hailes *Correspondence,*
Letter XXXVII, p. 122.

[4] *The Field of Flowden, A Des-*

criptive Poem, Edinburgh, 1768, 4°,
by Robert Colvill (d. 1788). It con-
tains dedicatory verses to "the Most
Ingenious And Learned Mr. Gray,
Now Republishing his Beautiful Lyric
Poems."

[5] William Robertson (1721–93),
the historian, Principal of Edinburgh
University.

wish you could prevail on your friend to try to recollect, or recover it, and send me another Copy by you.

I shall be very glad to see the List of Scottish Poets you mention, or anything else, which you judge to be curious; but what I chiefly want to recover are those fine old Historical Songs, which are only preserved in the memories of old People, &c; these are in so perishable a state that I apprehend it is nearly as much merit to retrieve them from that oblivion which they are falling into, as to compose them at first: I mean that the person | who does this will almost [p. 4.] deserve as well of the World as the original Composer; this merit your good Offices will certainly have, and none will be more ready to acknowledge it, than

Sir

Your most obliged

Humble Servant,

Tho⁵ Percy

PS/

I have returned Lord Hailes's Specimens of the *Godly Sangs &c,* having been formerly favoured with a Copy by himself, and I thought you might possibly wish (in that case,) to oblige some other friend with it.

NB. [p. 5.]

Should you have an opportunity of picking up another Copy of your Edition of Sʳ David Lindsay's Poems, reasonably, I should be glad if you would secure it for me.

I have most modern Scots Publications, viz.

Allan Ramsey's Works. 2 Vol.
Tea table Misc.
The Charmer.⁶
Blind Harry's Poem on Wallace. 4ᵗᵒ
John Barbour's Poem on Bruce. 4ᵗᵒ
&c

---

⁶ Followed by "2 Vol." deleted.

Indeed what I want, are rather Collections of the Common Historical ballads, &c such as are usually sold by Ballad Singers; or else
such as are only preserved in the memory of old People.

> *Address:* To Mr Paton
> at the Custom-House
> Edinburgh.

VI
From Paton[1]

[August 26, 1768]

Sir

I ought long ago to have acknowledged the Receipt of your agreeable Favours of 12th June, the Books came safe to hand with your
performance for which accept my Thanks.

Hitherto I have been greatly disappointed in receiving no satisfy-
ing Answers from my Friends applied to obtain some things for you
and my late Application to public Business has not a little restrain'd
me, but you may be assured whatever I can meet with of the Articles
mentioned in your last shall be transmitted.

It has not as yet been my Hap to meet with that Edition of Sir
David Lindsay's Works or any one worthy notice, but will proceed
in my Search, there are a Book or two by me of which I have dupli-
cates, these with what else I may meet with shall be sent up to
You, and in a Post or two hence a List of the Scottish Poets. I am
affraid very little dependance is to be made on *"Dempster"* [2] in his

---

[1] *Source:* British Museum, Add.
MS. 32332, f. 19.

[2] Thomas Dempster (*c.* 1579–
1625), Scots scholar, Latinist, biogra-
pher; professor at Toulouse, Nîmes,
and Bologna. *Historia Ecclesiastica
Gentis Scotorum: sive De Scriptori-*
bus Scotis, Bononiæ, 1627, 4°; edited
for the Bannatyne Club by D. Irving,
Edinburgh, 1829. Boadicea (Bunde-
vica) is included as the daughter of a
Scottish king and is credited with six
literary works.

Book "*Scotorum Ecclesiast. Historia,*" there appears to be too much of the Fabulous Credulity in his List of the Authors and their Works.

Mr Brown ^3 Librarian to the Faculty of Advocates some days ago gave me assurances that he was in Hopes to obtain ^4 | You the Use of [p. 2.] the Old M.SS. Poems ^5 in their Custody; of which Dr Blair would write you.

Please receive inclosed the "*Jew's Daughter,*" which only reach'd me t'other Day.

You should have been extremely welcome to [have] kept Lord Hailes's Specimen of the Godly Sangs &c^a and can provide you with one or two (in case) you desire to give them away.

T'other Week I chanc'd to meet with Mr Graham,^6 one of the Keepers of His Majesty's Liberary at the Queen's Palace, who told me he had made a purchase of a Collection of Poems a small thin 8° which were Scottish, but did not explain the Contents of the Book, if you are curious to see it I shall write to him under favour of your Cover, that you may enjoy a Sight of it, tho' I make no doubt from his Affability you may procure it on first Inquiry: this Book he bought in London for the Liberary:

I am

Revd Sir

Your most obedient humble Ser^t

GPaton

Customhouse Edinburgh
     26 August 1768

---

^3 Alexander Brown (d. 1801), librarian to the Faculty of Advocates from 1776 to 1794.

^4 Over "please turn over" at bottom of page.

^5 Almost certainly the "MS. quarto volume of old English Poetry" in the Advocates' Library referred to in the essay "On the Ancient Metrical Romances," *Reliques,* 1767, III, xxi–xxii. Scott, as late as 6 October 1800, offers to send Percy more detailed information about this MS. and to "point out much which in the cursory survey taken by the revd. and worthy Dr. Blair has been overlook'd or misapprehended," *Letters,* ed. H. J. C. Grierson and others, 1932–37, 12 vols., XII, 168.

^6 Richard Graham (*fl.* 1768). There is no record of him in the registers of the Royal Libraries. See also Percy-Hailes *Correspondence,* Appendix I, p. 155.

VII

From Percy[1]

Alnwick Castle, Septr 8.1768.

Sir,

I lose not a moment in acknowledging the kind favour of your last; and am much obliged to you both for your kind [2] Letter and for the curious old Song, it contained. Such favours are always acceptable. I thank you for all the hints contained in your letter, and shall endeavour to profit by them. We are all setting out for the South, where I hope I shall have the pleasure of hearing from you, when any more literary Curiosities fall in your way. I am at present going to spend a Month in Shropshire: but after my return to London [3] shall be perfectly happy to prosecute any Literary Disquisition you would wish.

> I am,
> Sir,
> Your obliged humble Servt
> Thomas Percy

VIII

From Paton[1]

[This letter of Autumn 1768 is missing.]

---

[1] *Source:* National Library of Scotland, MS. 29-5-8, Vol. I, f. 55.

[2] Over "obliging" deleted.

[3] The entry in Percy's *Journal* for 8 September reads: "Very busy packing up. . . . In the Evening I took leave of all my acquaintance." On 21 September Percy was in Shropshire ("I was made a Burgess of *Bridgnorth*"). By 10 October he was in London.

[1] Acknowledged in Letter IX.

IX
From Percy[1]

Northumberland House, Jan. 5. 1769[2]

Dear Sir

I received your very obliging Letter, containing the Catalogue of Dr Clarke's[3] Books, and promising a future Packet inclosed to Mr White[4] the bookseller: Whatever you are so good as to send me, will be always acceptable and be very gratefully received. As for the Auction, there are very few Articles in it that I want, if the following should be had upon very easy terms I should be glad to see them, but do not want them much. viz.

Pag. 49. N° 1173. Bartholinus[5] &c. 8vo (2^s or 2^s–6^d
    81.—2284. Hardyknute. 1st Edit. folio
        (I have already had a Transcript of all these MS. Notes[6]
    &c. but would give a small price[7] for the Original.
    81.—2295. Fordun.[8] 2 vol^s fol. (10^s or 12^s)

I am, Sir,
Your obliged Servant
Thomas Percy

---

[1] *Source:* National Library of Scotland, MS. 29-5-8, Vol. I, f. 51; printed in Maidment, pp. 3–4.

[2] Misdated 1768.

[3] John Clerk (1689–1757), physician in Edinburgh.

[4] Benjamin White (d. 1794), bookseller in London and sometime partner with John Whiston. See Nichols's *Literary Anecdotes of the Eighteenth Century*, III, 127.

[5] See Letter XII, n. 2, p. 22.

[6] See Letter I, n. 17, p. 2. Percy had secured a copy of the variations and notes added by Dr. Clerk. In *Reliques*, 1765, they were placed at the end of Volume III, pages 337–39, and in later editions at the end of Percy's own notes to "Hardyknute." See also Percy-Hailes *Correspondence*, pp. 42 and 49. Percy at some time acquired the copy of the folio edition of "Hardyknute," 1719, which is now in the Bodleian Library.

[7] Over "matter" deleted.

[8] *Joannis Forduni Scotichronicon cum continuatione Walteri Bower,* ed. Walter Goodall (1706?–66), Edinburgh, 1759, folio, 2 vols.

X
From Paton[1]

[January 21, 1769]

Dear Sir,

I was favour'd with yours of 5th Current would have answer'd it 'ere now, had I not been disabled by a sprain'd Leg and Fever out of both am slowly recovering.

I am hopefull M[r] Whyte has transmitted to you the Collection of Poems lately printed here:[2] what else may make a future appearance shall be immediately transmitted to your Hands.

D[r] Clark's Edition of Hardyknute is presently in my Custody, the Additional Stanzas are inserted in the Glasgow Edition[3] printed by Mess[rs] Foulis, whose Copy has more the Appearance of antique than this folio One printed by James Watson, which is elegantly executed, the Rarity of this Edition will encrease the Price tho' not so deserving as the Glasgow one in 4[to]. I shall observe your Directions about it and the other Books, only allow me to observe that the Price, put on *"Forduni Scotichronicon 2 Vol. fol.,"* of 10/– or 12/– is too low as I never found it sold under double that Money, it being a more

[p. 2.]   complete Book than Hearne's Edition.[4] | I had put into my Hands yesterday the Glasgow Edition of Hardyknute with M.SS. notes, a Criticism on it and some more Stanzas to the Poem, a Copy of which I shall with pleasure (if you chuse) transcribe for you and send alongst with any thing else I can pick up that may be entertaining.

---

[1] *Source:* British Museum, Add. MS. 32332. f. 20.

[2] *The Ancient and Modern Scots Songs, Heroic Ballads,* Edinburgh, 1769, 12°, collected by David Herd.

See Letters XI and XII, pp. 20, 22. [3] Glasgow, 1745, 1748, 4°. [4] Thomas Hearne (1678–1735), *Johannis de Fordun Scotichronicon genuinum,* Oxford, 1722, 8°.

Please to inform me if you design to publish a new Edition of your "Reliques of ancient Poetry" or when you intend it.

I am,

Revd Sir

Your most obedient Servt

GPaton

Edinburgh 21 January
1769

PS. Please excuse the Freedom used of my inclosing this Letter, to which be so good as cause give Currency to it.

Address: To The Reverend Dr Thomas Percy
Northumberland House
London

XI

From Percy[1]

Northumberland House, Feb.9.1769.

Sir,

I owe you my best thanks both for the obliging favour of your Letter and the very kind and valuable Present of your Book;[2] which is a very desirable Addition to my Collection of ancient Songs and Poems: I hope it will meet with all the incouragement it's merit deserves; so that you will soon be excited to give us another Volume of the same kind.—I am very glad (in particular) that you insert so many beautiful Fragments of Old Scots Ballads; because it will

---

[1] *Source:* National Library of Scotland, MS. 29-5-8, Vol. I, f. 56; printed in Maidment, pp. 9–12.

[2] See Letter X, n. 2, p. 18, and Letter XII, p. 22.

probably be a means of procuring the other stanzas to compleat them: for no Readers of Taste, that see your Collection, but will be desirous of furnishing you with the other parts, if they should hear of their
[p. 2.] being preserved in private hands | and thus your publication of an imperfect Fragment, will operate like an Advertisement to procure you the remainder.

As to your kind offer about lending me the MS. of Hardyknute: [3] if it should contain any very important improvements more than I published in my 2^d Edit. of the *Reliques of Ancient Poetry,* I should be glad to see it: otherwise I would not give you so much trouble.

As to *Forduni Chronicon,* I was in no great want of the Book: and this was the reason why I offered so low a price. I would perhaps go as far as 18^s or 21^s for a Copy, if it should fall in your way: otherwise I can do without it.

[p. 3.]   I shall be happy to make you some literary Return for your obliging favours and hope ere long I shall have an opportunity of that Sort. I am, with great Regard

Sir

Your very obliged

and faithful Servt

Thos Percy

PS/

I could wish you had accompanied your old Songs with a few historical or topographical Notes: [4] tho' I think you are so kind as to promise us something of this sort at the end of your next Volume: But I should think the Notes of each Volume, had better have been printed at the end of the several Volumes they belong to: this how-

---

[3] See Letter IX, n. 6, p. 17, and Letter XXIX, p. 39.

[4] This refers to the Advertisement (ix–x): ". . . the Publishers have still remaining in their custody imperfect copies and detached pieces of a great many more . . . intended for a subsequent volume: in which it is proposed to insert *notes* and *remarks*

. . . together with an ample Glossary. . . ." The whole work was recast for the second edition, *Ancient and Modern Scottish Songs,* Edinburgh, 1776, 8°, 2 vols. Over one hundred new poems were added, and there was extensive revision and rearrangement.

ever may be so contrived as to be done yet; it is but making your
Printer take care to give the Notes of each | Volume on Separate half- [p. 4.]
sheets, and then the Binder may place them at the end of the volumes
they respectively belong to.

Your Notes should be of four [5] kinds (Besides a General Glossary
to explain all the unusual Words and Phrases.)

1. To mention (where it can be done) the Authors of the several
Songs or Ballads, or at least their Antiquity, or any Tradition concerning them.
2. To explain the History or Story referred to in some of the Historical Ballads; where necessary.
3. To inform us in South-Britain, where the particular Scene or
Place lies, that is mentioned in some of the Pastoral Songs: as for
instance, in the old Sonnet intitled, The Broom of Cowdiknows:
it would be satisfactory to all curious Readers to be informed that
Cowdiknows [6] is the name of a very beautiful green hill that rises
near the ancient Abbey of Melrose not far from the banks of the *Tweed,*
in such a shire etc. etc.   query
4. Miscellaneous; either explanatory, or Digressive: particularly to
illustrate any Allusions to the old [7] Manners, Customs, Opinions, or
Idioms of the ancient Scotch Nation: these are now wearing out so
fast, that if not preserved in such publications as these, they will be
utterly unknown to posterity.

XII
From Paton[1]

[June 10, 1769]

Rever^d Sir

Some months ago I was favoured with Yours, which ought to have
been answered long ere this Time, but an accidental Sprain and

[5] Over "three" deleted.
[6] Cowdenknows, near Earlston in
Berwickshire. *Songs,* 1769, p. 17;
1776, I, 181. Percy's location is ten-
tative.

[7] Over "ancient" deleted.
[1] *Source:* British Museum, Add.
MS. 32332, ff. 22–23.

other Distresses prevented me till now, when I beg Leave to inform You that by a Friend, who goes to London by Sea next Week you shall have

    1. Bartholinus [2] de Morbis Biblicis 12°

    2. Collect. Varia de rebus Gestis Gul. Wallace [3] 12°

    3. Ross's Fortunate Sheperdess [4] a Tale in the Scottish Dialect 8°

which if you think worthy to give a Place amongst your Collection, be pleased to accept of them.

You did me more Honour than intitled to, by reckoning me as the Publisher of the Volume of Songs [5] sent you: I never knew any thing of the Work, till it was to be usher'd into the World and then used the Freedom of transmitting a Copy to You, as I shall be always ready to hand you any thing that may be any how connected with your Performance, which does exceed all of the Kind the Nation has been obliged with.

Mr Burt [6] the Publisher I am a Stranger to, but an Acquaintance of his being with me when I received your Letter he beg'd a Sight of your most Judicious Remarks and Improvements, which are to be [p. 2.] observed in the second Volume, for which he is | making collections; for your Observations he exprest particular Thanks and would be singularly obliged for any more as your Convenience will permit.

I have no Inclination, nor will the Attention to the Duty in the Business of the Revenue permit me to be concerned much in any publications any further than by a transient Amusement after the Fatigues of the Office. It has not yet hapned that I could procure you

[2] Thomas Bartholinus (1616–80), *De morbis Biblicis miscellanea medica,* Francofurti, 1672, 8°.

[3] *De gestis Gulielmi Vallae, Scotiae olim Custodis, collectanea varia . . . , Collectore Roberto Sibbald,* ed. A. Symson, Edinburgh, 1705, 8°.

[4] Alexander Ross (1699–1784), *The Fortunate Shepherdess. A Pastoral Tale; In Three Cantos, in the Scotish Dialect. By Mr. Alexander Ross School-Master at Lochlee. To*

which is added a few Songs by the same Author, Aberdeen, 1768, 4°. See *The Scottish Works of Alexander Ross,* M.A., ed. Margaret Wattie (Scottish Text Society), Edinburgh, 1938.

[5] For "Publisher" as used here the modern term would be "editor." The volume in question is Herd's *Scots Songs:* see Letter X, n. 2, p. 18.

[6] Evidently a mishearing of Herd (pronounced Hurd).

a Copy of Sir David Lindsay's Works, in my Search I saw an Edition printed at London 1581 in 4to. The Title Page of which bears "first turned and made perfect English [7] &c^a^ " but it does not contain all his Works and the Language (to me at least) appears misapplied and not so nervous as in the Scotish Dialect.

I saw lately in a Gentleman's Possession a large Folio containing not only many valuable Original Papers relating to the Transactions in this Country during the grand Rebellion in Charles's Time, but also a number of Tracts, Poems &^a^ all M.S.S. collected by Sir ―――― Lauder [8] of Fountainhall one of our Senators of the College of Justice; this Collection as I have no hopes of making myself possessor of, yet shall attempt to get it deposited in the Liberary belonging to the Faculty of Advocates, where public Access can be got to it. The World suffer'd much in the Dispersion of that Knight's Liberary, his Successor ignorant of it's value, not only allowed his M.SS. Ob- [p. 3.] servations and some of his Works amounting to several Porter's Burdens to perish for Snuff Paper, but more were destroyed otherways: amongst which were many Things not now to be recovered.

I shall write you alongst with the small Parcel and will be extremely glad to hear from you at your Leisure.

> I am
> Revd Sir
> Your most obedient humble
> Servant GPaton

Customhouse Edinburgh
   10 June 1769

Docket: Mr Geo. Paton   Edinb^r^ 1769

[7] *A Dialogue betweene Experience and a Courtier, . . . First turned and made perfect English: . . . Imprinted at London, An. Dom. 1581.*

[8] Sir John Lauder of Fountainhall (1644–1722). The bulk of his surviving MSS. are in the National Library of Scotland. The most important were published by the Bannatyne Club: *Historical Selections . . . 1680–86*, Edinburgh, 1837, 4°; *Historical Observes . . .* , Edinburgh, 1840, 4°; *Historical Notices . . .* , Edinburgh, 1848, 4°, 2 vols.

XIII
From Percy[1]

Alnwick Castle, July 15.1769.

Dear Sir,

Your kind Letter and obliging Present of the 3 books came safe to hand, and are intitled to my most grateful Acknowledgments: they (as all your kind Presents ever are) form a very valuable addition to my small Collection. I shall not rest till I endeavour to pick up something that may not be altogether unacceptable to you. When I return to London in the Autumn I shall intreat your acceptance of two volumes[2] 8ᵛᵒ that will be then published by a friend of mine, and beg you will let me know by a Line where and how I can forward them to you. I should be glad if you would send me another Copy of the *Volume of Songs,* you lately obliged me with; they are for a friend, from whom I will transmit the Price as you shall direct, or rather I will desire my friend Dʳ Blair to repay you. I should be glad [p. 2.] if they could be sent to me here, | or left (directed for me at Alnwick Castle) at Mʳˢ Parker's at the Post Office in Newcastle

I am
Dear Sir
Your most obliged
humble Servant
Thoˢ Percy

PS/
I am very glad that a 2ᵈ Volume of the Old Songs is intended.

Address: To George Paton Esq
at the Custom House
in
Edinburgh

[1] *Source:* National Library of Scotland, MS. 29-5-8, Vol. I, f. 57; printed in Maidment, pp. 12–13.

[2] See Letter XXVIII, n. 2, p. 38.

XIV
From Paton[1]

[July 24, 1769]

Dear Sir

I am favoured this Day with yours of 15th Current and am happy that the Books have reached you, could I in any manner contribute to the addition of your Collection, pray do me the favour with your Convenience as serve me with a List of any Scots or English Books that may appear here and that seldom offer in England, it shall give me a very agreeable pleasure to pick them up for you.

I return you Thanks for your kind Intention and will most thankfully pay any Work you're pleased to recommend or have any Concern in, or published by your Friends, to be possessed of them will make me happy.

You may depend on having a *Copy of the Songs* sent you by the first Waggon or Carrier from this for Newcastle, and shall give the Person Directions to leave the small Parcel Either at Alnwick or at Mrs Parker's in Newcastle: The Book you will be kind enough to accept of and present to your Friend.

When I see the Publisher of the Songs shall inquire when he intends to publish another Volume and will write you soon.

I am
Dear Sir
Your most obedient Servant
GPaton

Customhouse Edinburgh
24 July 1769

[1] *Source:* British Museum, Add. MS. 32332, f. 24.

XV

From Paton[1]

[July 31, 1769]

Dear Sir

I sent off your Volume of Songs by the Waggon for Newcastle, with a Direction to leave it at Mrs Parker's and suppose it may be there by tomorrow or Wednesday.

Please receive inclosed a Country Discription of a Courtship and Wedding, which was never printed.[2] I copied it while a Young Lady sung it lately and hope to send you another in a Post or two hence.

I beg your Excuses at present but will write soon and am

Dear Sir
Your most obedient Servt
GPaton

Customh° Edinburgh
31 July 1769

XVI

From Percy[1]

Alnwick Castle, Aug.18.1769.

Dear Sir,

I received very safe the Volume of Scottish Songs, which you were so good as to send me and am extremely obliged to you for

[1] *Source:* Harvard College Library, bMS Eng 893 (124B).
[2] A version entitled "Patie and Maggie's Courtship" almost identical with Paton's is preserved in David Herd's manuscripts (British Museum, Add. MS. 22311, ff. 79–80). The manuscript versions are more idio- matic than those printed in Herd's *Ancient and Modern Scottish Songs,* Edinburgh, 1776, 2 vols., II, 188, and Robert Jamieson's *Popular Ballads and Songs,* Edinburgh, 1806, 2 vols., I, 309–14.
[1] *Source:* National Library of Scotland, MS. 29-5-8, Vol. I, f. 58.

the same but am very much ashamed to trespass so much upon your Good Nature as I have done on this and former accounts. I shall be extremely glad to see the 2ᵈ Volume of Scottish Songs, when published, and beg you will purchase two Copies for me, but not unless you let me repay you for this and your former disbursements: I am with great Truth

Dear Sir
Your most obedient
and obliged Servant
Tho. Percy

XVII

From Percy[1]

[This letter of 14 November 1769 is missing.]

XVIII

From Paton[1]

[December 9, 1769]

Dear Sir

Fourteen Days ago I was favoured with Yours of 14ᵗʰ past when to my great uneasiness I found the two first Books past in the Auction, but if you incline will recover the first vizᵗ. Eginharti Vita [2] &ᶜ as an Acquaintance of mine purchased it, the second Book Sir R. Grey's [3] Vel. Paterculus sold for a Trifle to some unknown person, but took Care to secure *Ardlington's Apuleius*,[4] which shall be sent up

---

[1] Acknowledged in Letter XVIII.

[1] *Source:* British Museum, Add. MS. 32332, f. 25.

[2] Einhard (*c.* 770–840), *Vita et Gesta Karoli Magni*, Cologne, 1521, 4°.

[3] Sir Robert Le Grys (d. 1635).

See transcript of title page, Letter XLIII, p. 63.

[4] William Adlington (*fl.* 1566), *The XI bookes of the Golden Asse . . . Translated out of Latin*, 1566, 4°.

to you in a Parcel either for Mr Davies [5] or Mr Payne [6] Booksellers, and please let me know as soon as convenient if I may procure *Eginhartus* to be put up with Apuleius: both which you will do me the Favour of accepting from me.

The second Volume of the Scots Songs &^c will not be sent to the press till the Spring, but how soon it is published I will embrace the opportunity of transmitting the Copies to you.

I beg you will pardon the Freedom I use in putting the inclosed [p. 2.] to an acquaintance of mine under your Cover | to which please cause give Currency, as I can obtain no frank Covers here.

With pleasure wait your Answer, which will much oblige

Dear Sir

Your most obedient humble

Servt   GPaton

Customhouse Edinburgh
    9 December 1769
    Eginhartus has the Plate

Address: To The Reverend Dr Thomas Percy
        Northumberland House
        London

XIX

From Percy [1]

Northumberland House, Decr 20. 1769.

Dear Sir,

I received the very obliging favour of your Letter, and am glad you

---

[5] Thomas   Davies   (1712?–85), bookseller in Russell Street, Covent Garden, and author. See Nichols's *Literary Anecdotes*, VI, 421–43.

[6] "Honest Tom Payne" (1719–99), bookseller. His shop at Mews-gate,

Westminster, is mentioned in *Literary Anecdotes*, VI, 440.

[1] *Source:* National Library of Scotland, MS. 29-5-8, Vol. I, f. 59; printed in Maidment, pp. 14–15.

have secured me *Adlington's Apuleius;* but I cannot think of receiving it from you on any other terms than that of repaying you what it cost in the Auction. I must therefore beg to be informed how much I am indebted to you for this and other books you have been so good as to transmit to me: otherwise you will render it impossible for me ever to trouble you again.

Incapable as I am of making you any other returns but [2] those of a meer literary nature, I can by no means trespass upon your good nature in the manner in which your benevolence would invite me: but if you will point out any Services of the same literary kind by which I can return your obliging favours, you will then encourage me to apply to you again on similar occasions | to those by which you [p. 2.] have already rendered me

Dear Sir

Your obliged and most obedient Servant

Tho[s] Percy

PS/

I am obliged to you for the offer of procuring me *Eginhartus,* but as the present possessor [3] probably would not wish to be deprived of his purchase, I would by no means rob him of it.

Apuleius may be sent in any parcell which the Edinburgh Booksellers have to remit to our Book-sellers in London; any of whom would probably convey it safely, if it was directed to me at Northumberland House; and by the same Channel I must beg to remit you what I am in your debt, of which you will please to inform me.

---

[2] Over "than" deleted.   [3] Over "purchaser" deleted.

XX
From Paton[1]

[December 26, 1769]

Dear Sir

I am obliged with Your Favours of the 20th Current and beg Leave to acquaint You that *Ardlington's*[2] *Apuleius,* is put up in a Box for M[r] Payne Bookseller at the Meuse,[3] who I hope will transmit the Parcel to Northumberland-house how soon it comes to his Hand, as Cap[t] Farmer[4] of the Edinburgh[5] sails for London one of these Days.

How soon the Possessor of *Eginhartus* returns to Town I shall inquire if he will part with the Book and advise you of it.

It gives me great Concern to be in Danger of procuring your Displeasure, and denied the Opportunity of the Pleasure of serving you, which I beg you will alter your Intention of, as the few things sent are Trifles, so hope to enjoy future Occasions of serving you and oblige

Dear Sir
Your most obedient Serv[t]
GPaton

Customhouse Edinburgh
    26 December 1769

Docket: G. Paton Edinburgh
        26 Dec[r] 1769

[1] *Source:* British Museum, Add. MS. 32332, f. 27.

[2] Paton's misspelling of "Adlington" (see Letter XVIII *supra*) may represent his pronunciation.

[3] See Letter XVIII, n. 6, p. 28.

[4] Peter Farmer (*fl.* 1771), shipmaster at Leith.

[5] The "Edinburgh" was a fast-sailing brigantine of 180 tons burden, carrying goods and passengers between Leith and London.

XXI

From Percy[1]

Northumberland House, 7 May. 1770

Sir

I have had a Gentleman from Edinburgh call on me lately once or twice; but as he did not leave his Name, I could not discover who he was; I shall be very sorry if I find it was you, that you would not inform me where I could wait on you. I am now leaving Town for a Month, at my return I should be glad to find a Line from you to inform me how I can convey a few Books to you in the most safe and easy Manner; and am, with the greatest Esteem

Sir

Your very faithful

and obliged Servant

Tho[s] Percy

PS/
Pray when may one hope to see the 2[d] Vol. of the Songs?

XXII

From Paton[1]

[May 14, 1770]

Rev[d] Sir

Hurry of Publick Business in the Revenue here be assured is the only Reason of my Silence to your obliging Letter by the Favor of D[r] Blair.

[1] *Source:* National Library of Scotland, MS. 29-5-8, Vol. I, f. 60.

[1] *Source:* British Museum, Add. MS. 32332, f. 28.

Two days ago my worthy good Friend Mr Davidson transmitted me your Agreeables of 7th Current,[2] informing me of a Gentleman calling of you, which you suspected to have been me, it was not for it never has been my good Fortune, to have enjoyed the Length of My Chain from the Desk to London since I enter'd into the Customhouse, but once, and that was before I enjoyed the Happyness of your Correspondence, had that Indulgence been or shall again be shewn me, You may be assured, no Time should have been lost of paying my most dutifull Thanks of Gratitude to You for Favors, and the repeated Testimony of your unmerited Regard, by the kind Offer made me in your two last Letters, which Offer I not only shall welcome but be proud of giving any Work in which you may be concerned, a Place amongst the few Books in my Possession.

I wish to have a good Errand to the great City to advance my small Living, when it should be my Desire to have your promoting Hand in assisting me thereto by Advice and Interest.

As you signify Your leaving London for some Time I shall give Directions to a Friend in London to call at Northumberland House, [p. 2.] and receive any thing you have to send down here for any | of your Friends or me and he will take particular Care of them, as it must afford you too much Trouble to give them by your Servant into any of the Booksellers with you, who correspond with their Brethren in Trade here, who all know me well; Parcels come here by every Scots' Ship.

I am sorry it is not in my Power to acquaint you when the Second Volumes of the Songs [3] will be published as the Gentleman who collects them had not last Winter procured a sufficient Quantity, and the Promises of more being so great he procrastinated the Exhibition of a Second Volume for a longer Time than at first he intended: but

---

[2] It seems that Percy's letter of 7 May was sent in Blair's packet and reached Paton through John Davidson (d. 1797) of Haltree, Writer to the Signet. See p. 31 *supra*.

[3] See an account of this volume in Hans Hecht's *Songs from David Herd's Manuscripts*, pp. 65–68, and see also Appendix II.

you may depend on't how soon it appears, I shall immediately forward it to You.

                I am
                    Revd Sir
                        Your most obedient and obliged humble
                                Servant
                                GPaton

Customhouse Edinburgh
    14 May 1770

    Docket: Mr Paton
        14 May 1770

XXIII
From Paton[1]

[May 21, 1770]

Dear Sir

   I have transmitted this to an Acquaintance James Robertson,[2] who presently resides in Westminster; he will be so good as take the Charge of any thing you intend to send to Scotland and thro' his Care hope these will come safe to hand, in Case you have anything for other Friends here they may be put in the same Parcel and shall see all properly dilivered here.

---

[1] *Source:* British Museum, Add. MS. 32332, f. 30.
[2] James Robertson (*fl.* 1793), "a misfortunate man," was married to a relative of Paton's. See a letter of Paton to Dr. William Cuming, 29 November 1779 (National Library of Scotland, Adv. MS. 29-5-7, Vol. II, n.f.). See Letter LXXXVII, n. 4, p. 128.

I wrote you some Posts ago to which refer you.

I am

Dear Sir

Your most obedient Servant

GPaton

Customhouse Edinburgh

21 May 1770

Address: To The Reverend Doctor Thomas Percy

at His Grace The Duke of Northumberland's

Northumberland House

London

Docket: Mr Paton

21 May. 1770

XXIV

From Percy[1]

Alnwick Castle in Northumberland

6th Augst 1770.

Dear Sir,

I have been so little in Town for some Months past, that I was unfortunately out of the way when your friend called for the Books, and as he neither left any direction nor did you favour me with any, where to find him, I had it not in my power to forward them to him; but if you will be pleased to give me another Line, with a Standing Direction where to send the books to any friend of yours,

[1] *Source:* National Library of Scotland, MS. 29-5-8, Vol. I, f. 61.

when I return to London, I will forward them in any Manner you shall appoint, and am Dear Sir

> Your most obedient
> Humble Servant
> Tho⁸ Percy

XXV
From Paton¹

[August 21,1770]

Dear Sir

I was some Posts ago obliged with your agreeable Favours from Alnwick Castle and shall be overjoyed to have a Share of your satisfactory Correspondence as the avocation from more necessary Affairs may permit.

The Young Man in London being married to a Relation of mine I desired him to call as he past Northumberland House for the Parcel you was so kind as promise me, but unfortunately you was abroad, but there is no Matter, for he will call any time this ensuing Winter, and then take Charge of it by sending same to Leith in one of our London Trading Ships.

I have been promised a Sight of "Sir David Lindsay's "Interludes" ² 4ᵗᵒ. This is not amongst his other Works usually printed in a small size: the Gentleman regretts it is imperfet, but tells me it breathes the most severe Satyre against the Romish Clergy, as it is generally allowed that the Knight's Poems sowed the Seeds of the Reformation in this Country; I am also promised a reading of his

---

¹ *Source:* British Museum, Add.   Edinburgh, 1602, 4° (published by
MS. 32332, ff. 32–33.   Robert Charteris).
² *Ane Satyre of the Thrie Estaits,*

"*Poem on Cardinal Beton's Death*":[3] if you are desirous to see
[p. 2.] either | or both of them, I shall be proud of this Opportunity to
gratify your Curiosity as probably these have never past thro' your
Hands; which after perusal you may be pleased to send them back to
me by the New Castle Carrier again if you're to pass any Weeks in
Northumberland.

I should be glad to know if his Grace of Northumberland is possessed of a Copy of "*Andersoni*[4] *Select. Numismat. et Diplomat.
Scotiæ fol*" published by Mr Thos Ruddiman who prefixt a very
learn'd Introduction to this Work; but as there are some old Family
Charters, not inserted in that Collection, which were printed for
the Curiosity's sake, if His Grace inclines I will endeavour to pick up
one or two of these so as they may be inserted into the Collection
made by Mr Anderson.

I am with the greatest Respect

Dear Sir

Your most obedient Servant

GPaton

Customhouse Edinburgh
  21 August 1770

Docket: Mr Paton
  21 August 1770

---

[3] David   Beaton   (1494–1546),
Cardinal and Archbishop of St. Andrews, *The tragical death of David
Beaton, Bishoppe of sainct Andrewes
in Scotland. . . . Imprinted at London, by John Daye, and William
Seres,* 1547?, 8°. See discussion of a
conjectural parent edition and of early
editions in *The Bibliography of Sir
David Lindsay,* by D. Hamer, *The
Library,* Fourth Series, X, 5-30, and

Works (Scottish Text Society), ed.
D. Hamer, 1936, IV, 20.

[4] James   Anderson   (1662–1728),
Writer to the Signet. *Selectus Diplo-
matum & Numismatum Scotiæ The-
saurus,* Edinburgh, 1739, folio. Ruddiman's "Praefatio" or Introduction
was translated and published at Edinburgh, 1773, 8°. See Letter XLVI,
n. 4, p. 65.

XXVI
From Paton[1]

[This letter of 1 October 1770 is missing.]

XXVII
From Paton[1]

[November 5, 1770]

Dear Sir

Having procured from a Friend out of a Collection in folio of Sundry Pamphlets the first Edition of Hardyknute [2] I take the opportunity of transmitting it to you, as you seem'd fond to be possessed of a Copy, if this is agreeable you will do me the Favour of giving it a place amongst your Collection: let me know what else you may have a Fancy for here and if I can meet with them shall be at your Service.

The second Volume of the Scot's Songs is not published when it appears you may depend on the Copies required, this has been retarded from unforseen Accidents.

> I am
> > Dear Sir
> > > Your most obedient Servant
> > > GPaton

Customhouse Edinburgh
   5th November 1770

---

[1] Acknowledged in Letter XXVIII.
[1] *Source:* British Museum, Add. MS. 32332, f. 34.

[2] See Letter IX, p. 17 and Letter XXIX, n. 2, p. 39.

Docket: Mr Paton
5 Novr 1770

Address: To The Reverend Dr Thomas Percy
Northumberland House
London

XXVIII

From Percy[1]

Easton Maud^t Northamptonshire
10 Novr 1770

Dear Sir,

I received your obliging Letter of 1 Octr accompanied with a Catalogue of *Bell's* Auction &c. I have looked it carefully over, but do not find any thing that I particularly want at present.—

A Copy of *the Northern Antiquities* [2] has lien ready for you packed up at Northumberland House these 5 Months, and lies now in the Porter's Lodge directed *to Mr Paton, to be called for:* if you will order any person to call for Mr Paton's Parcel, without further Questions, it will be delivered to him.—I am at present confined in the country with ill health but remain   Sir

Your most obedient
Humble Servant
Thos Percy

Address: To Geo. Paton Esq
at the Custom House
Edinburgh

[1] *Source:* National Library of Scotland, MS. 29-5-8, Vol. I, f. 62.
[2] *Northern Antiquities: or, A Description of the Manners, Customs, Religion and Laws of the Ancient Danes . . . Translated from Mons. Mallet's Introduction à l'Histoire de Dannemarc,* London, 1770, 8°, 2 vols.

XXIX
From Percy[1]

Easton Maudit, 17th of Novr 1770

Dear Sir,

I wrote to you a few days ago, and the very next post brought me your obliging Letter accompanied with the curious Copy of the first Edition of *Hardiknute* than which you could not have made me a more acceptable present. Receive my best acknowledgments for so obliging a mark of your attention and regard. I should be glad if you could inform me when the 2^d and inlarged Edition of that beautiful Poem appeared:[2] Whether in a small Separate publication, or in the *Evergreen,* published in 1724; (wherein this Poem is printed with the latest improvements.)—You will probably be able, without much difficulty to ascertain this point.

—I believe, in my last I mentioned that any friend of yours that would inquire of the porter at Northumberland House for a parcel directed for Mr Paton, would receive it ready packed up for you. I am still detained by ill health[3] in the Country, but a Line may be directed for me under Cover to His Grace at Northumberland House as usual. I am, Dear Sir

Your obliged Servant
Thos Percy

---

[1] *Source:* National Library of Scotland, MS. 29-5-8, Vol. I, f. 63; printed in Maidment, pp. 15–17.

[2] See Letter I, n. 17, p. 2. Later editions are London, 1740, 4° (Dodsley); Glasgow, 1745 and 1748, small 4° (Foulis).

[3] A few hours after writing this letter, Percy lost his child Anne (b. 18 March 1760). See his *Journal* for 18 November.

XXX
From Percy

[This letter of late December 1770 is missing.]

XXXI
From Paton[1]

[January 3, 1771]

Dear Sir

I was several Posts ago favoured with Yours and have been so
much occupied with the Business of the Revenue that I could not
find as much Time as to make you an Answer, which you must please
prolong an Excuse to me. Having got a Catalogue which contains a
good Number of rare Books to be sold here I use the Freedom of
transmitting a Copy to You, and shall be fond of having Notice
should it contain any Book you or any Friend desire to have.

I beg you will accept of my best Thanks for Your Present of the
Northern Antiquities, which came to hand this day, wishing you the
Compliments of the Season with many happy Returns. I am

Dear Sir

Your most obedient and obliged
humble Servant
GPaton

Customhouse Edinburgh
3 January 1771

[1] Acknowledged in Letter XXXI.   [1] *Source:* British Museum, Add.
MS. 32332, f. 36.

Address: To The Reverend Dr Thomas Percy
        Northumberland House
        London

Docket: Mr Paton
       Jany^y 3 1771

XXXII

From Paton[1]

[October 17, 1772]

Dear Sir

It is long since I ought to have acknowledged your kind Favours of the sweet Poem The Hermit of Warkworth,[2] which reach'd me long ago.

I am desired by the Collector and Publisher of *the Collection of Scots Songs,* the first Volume whereof I sent you on its Publication, that he has now got together such a number as will make up another Volume, but the Share of Business that he is engaged in will not admit of the Care of publishing it, so requested me to write you if you would do it,[3] that I should get the Manuscript from him and transmit as you shall be pleased to instruct me: which when reviewed what necessary Information &c^a should be communicated I shall be

---

[1] *Source:* Harvard College Library, bMS Eng 893 (124C).

[2] *The Hermit of Warkworth. A Northumberland Ballad. In Three Fits or Cantos,* London, 1771, 4°. It was published on 21 May: see the *Public Advertiser.* Percy wrote it at the request of the Duchess of North-

umberland. (See Percy to Rev. William Jessop, 6 April 1784, Bodleian, MS. Percy, C. 1.) Proof sheets of the first edition, corrected in Percy's hand, are preserved in the Sterling Memorial Library at Yale.

[3] See Appendix II, p. 171.

very glad to have your Sentiments on this Subject when most convenient.

You will please to receive inclosed a Copy of an ancient Charter wherein the ancient Family of Percy are recorded, the Original I have seen and in fine Order for the distant Period in which it was written.

I should be glad to know if ever you saw a Copy of *Sir David Lindsay's* (*of the Mount*) *Satyres* [4] 4to which contributed to the Rise of the Reformation in this Country, it is extremely scarce, can find no Copy of it in any public Liberary here altho' it was printed: you will observe the Reason of it's Scarcity pointed out by Lindsay of Pitscottie's History [5] p. 202 Fol. Edit.—I observe that Rowe [6] in his M.SS. History of the Church of Scotland attributes the Reformation to the above Satyre as also to *Wedderburne's Psalms and Godly Ballatis,*[7] which I take to be the Book I sent you a Sight of, it is the second Edition, as I have by me a Sheet of the same Book but does

[p. 2.] not correspond with the perfect Copy you saw. I find that Sir David wrote another Poem intituled *The History of Squyre Meldrum,*[8] which is omitted in all the modern Editions of his Works, altho' has been twice printed once in the old Edition of his Works by Henry Charteris at Edinburgh 4to and in a small 12°.

It will be kind to have your Opinion whether a neat Edition of all our Scots Poets carefully printed in pocket volumes might not be acceptable to the Publick, the Impression not numerous, I should think every Poet whether M.SS. or already printed ought to make part of the Collection.

I hope this Winter shall furnish me with an Opportunity of send-

---

[4] See Letter XXV, n. 2, p. 35.
[5] Robert Lindsay of Pitscottie in East Fife (1500–65?), *The History of Scotland; . . . By Robert Lindesay of Pitscottie,* Edinburgh, 1728, folio; Glasgow, 1749, 12°. See Letter XXXIV, p. 45.
[6] See Letter III, n. 13, p. 8.
[7] See Letter III, n. 13, p. 8, and Letter I, n. 18, p. 3.
[8] The earliest *extant* edition is: *The*

Historie of Ane Nobil And Wailzeand Squyer, William Meldrum, vmquhyle Laird of Cleische and Bynnis . . . , Imprentit at Edinburgh be Henrie Charteris, 1594, 4°. It is included in the table of contents in H. Charteris's edition of the *Warkis,* Edinburgh, 1582, 4°, but does not form part of the volume. Other editions are: Edinburgh, 1610, 4°; 1634, 8°; 1683, 12°; Glasgow, 1696, 18°.

ing you some things, which are to be reprinted here, and with your Convenience shall be glad to know to what place I may address them for you.—Be so good as inform whether, *The Northumberland Household Book*[9] is [to] be sold and where to be got, I am extremely anxious to see it.

If you desire to see the Chamberlain of Scotland's Accounts[10] for the Years 1329. 1330 and 1331 I would send them under Frank Covers as it does not consist of many Sheets.

I shall be obliged to you for your Answer and am

> Dear Sir
>
> Your most obliged and obedient
>
> humble Serv[t]
>
> GPaton

Customhouse Edinburgh
17 October 1772

XXXIII

From Percy[1]

Oct[r] 27. 1772. Easton Maudit
Near Castle Ashby Northamptonshire.

Dear Sir,

I cannot defer thanking you for the kind favour of your Letter and valuable Present of the ancient Charter, which were extremely

---

[9] Edited by Percy and issued privately with preface and notes, 1770, as *The Regulations and Establishment of the Houshold of Henry Algernon Percy, the Fifth Earl of Northumberland, at his Castles of Wresill and Lekinfield in Yorkshire. Begun Anno Domini M.D.XII. London Printed* M.DCC.LXX. The half title has "Houshold-Book."

[10] *Accounts of the Chamberlain of Scotland in . . . 1329, 1330 and 1331*, ed. John Davidson, Edinburgh, 1771, 4⁰.

[1] *Source:* National Library of Scotland, MS. 29-5-8, Vol. I, f. 64; printed in Maidment, pp. 17–19.

acceptable. If the Publisher of the *Collection of Scots Songs* would send up by some safe hand his Collections for the 2^d Vol. for my inspection and perusal, I will see what can be done, let them be forwarded to me at Northumberland House.

I wish we had correct and neat Editions of all the best old Scottish Poets, but it is an undertaking that requires some little Consideration: I should be glad to concur towards it in any shape.

[p. 2.]   I never saw the old pieces of Lindsay which you mention: they must be curious.

—I wish it was in my power to give you a Copy of the Northumberland Houshold Book, as they will not be sold; but it is not as yet in my power: His Grace printed few and the 3 or 4, which he allowed me to send to Edinburgh, were chiefly to such as he had some particular reason of his own for sending them to. Should it hereafter be in my power, I shall be happy to place a Copy in the hands of a Gentleman to whom I am so much obliged for similar favours.

I am
Dear Sir
Your most obedient Servant
Tho. Percy

PS/

Inclose any Packet to me under Cover to *The Earl of Sussex*, at this place: only add a large P on the back of the Cover.[2]

Address: To Geo. Paton Esq
at the Custom House
Edinburgh

[2] After "Direct" deleted.

XXXIV

From Paton[1]

[November 21, 1772]

Dear Sir

I am extremely happy to learn that my last reached you, should have answered your Favours of 27 past but was called unexpectedly to the Country to wait of a Friend who was dangerously ill.

It will be about the beginning of the Year ere I can get the Collections for the 2ᵈ Volume of the Songs sent to Northumberland House as it is presently in the Country on geting Additions made to it.

I am happy that you approve of the Scheme of publishing the best *Scottish Poets,* but find it will indeed require Time, Consideration &c. in the meantime shall endeavour to pick up as many as I can of which will use the ffreedom to advise you as these may occurr to me, after which some Scheme may fall [?] on for publishing some as a Tryal.

I delivered Mʳ Davidson t'other day Pitscottie's History of Scotland fol. Edition for your acceptance, please look into page 202 for *Sir D. Lindsay's Satyres,* the fate it met with here,[2] as I wrote my Copy is imperfect, but am in hopes thro' the Means of my good Friend Richᵈ Gough [3] Esqʳ Author of *"Anecdotes of British Topography &ᶜ* 4ᵗᵒ " to get it's defects supplied from the Bodleian Liberary

---

[1] *Source:* Harvard College Library, bMS Eng 893 (124D).

[2] "Ffarder they maid ane act that Schir Dawid Lyndsayis buike sould be condemnid and bruntt and so they performitt the same and bruntt is as ze sall heir efterwart." See *The Historie and Cronicles of Scotland . . . Written and Collected by Robert Lindsay of Pitscottie,* ed. by Æneas J. C. Mackay (Scottish Text Society), Edinburgh, 1899, 2 vols., II, 141. D.

Hamer discusses whether the proscribed work was *Ane Satyre of the Thrie Estaitis* or *The Monarche* or *The Tragedie of the Late Cardinal Beaton,* in "The Bibliography of Sir David Lindsay," *The Library,* Fourth Series, X, 17–20.

[3] Richard Gough (1735–1809), Director of the Society of Antiquaries 1771–97, *Anecdotes of British Topography,* London, 1768, 4º. The MSS. of his correspondence with Paton are

[p. 2.] where I | suspect it is, but shall be shortly more truely informed of it afterwards on his Return to London.

Mr Davidson shewed me Your Copy of *"Peblis at the Play"* [4] first spare hour I've will read it over &^{c}. I am pretty certain you will find many of Sir David Lindsay's Poems [5] in the Collection by *Banantyne* to be transmitted you [6] from this, and believe part if not the whole of his Satyres may be in that M.S.S. of Banantyne. I suspect that *"Peblis at the Play"* may be his performance as he lived in the County of Tweedale at *Mount* [7] *near Skirling* but I may be mistaken.—If you meet with such a small Book as *"Scotland's Complaint* [8] *&^{c}"* you'l find mention made of several old Songs or Poems there which we now know nothing of. I have searched in vain for this Book.

I return you my most gratefull thanks for your kind generous Favour about the Household Book, but beg you will not put yourself to any trouble on my Account.

Please receive inclosed the *"Battle of Corrichie"* [9] and *"Discription of Halow Fair"* [10] by a Young Lad of 18 years, he intends to imitate Gaw. Douglass by translating the Eclogues and Georgics,

in the National Library of Scotland, Adv. MSS. 29-5-6, 29-5-7.

[4] "Your Copy" was Percy's own *transcript.* He had discovered *Peblis to the Play* in the Maitland Folio MS. by 1761. (See *Letters of William Shenstone,* ed. Marjorie Williams, Oxford, 1939, p. 598), but it was first published by John Pinkerton (1758–1826), in *Select Scotish Ballads,* 1783, 2 vols., II, 1–14. Pinkerton admits that he owed his knowledge of the poem to Percy: "to whom alone the reader is beholden for it," and acknowledges "the politeness, peculiar to himself, with which the communication of this poem was made," p. xi.

[5] See Letter XLII, n. 2, p. 61.

[6] See Letter XXXVI, p. 52.

[7] The Mount is in the parish of Monimail in Fife, about three miles west of Cupar.

[8] See Letter LXX, n. 3, p. 104.

[9] *The Battle of Corichie.* It appeared in the *Scots Weekly Magazine,* July 1772, where it is attributed to "one Forbes schoolmaster at Maryculter, Dee-side." See Ritson's *Scotish Songs,* 1794, II, 14, and J. Maidment's *Scotish Ballads and Songs,* Edinburgh, 1868, 8°, 2 vols., I, 215.

[10] "Hallow-Fair," by Robert Fergusson (1750–74), student at St. Andrews and law clerk in Edinburgh. See Letter XXXVII, n. 2, p. 53, and LXXVI, n. 3, p. 113.

and then publishing the Aeneid with it, but of this afterwards. If anything material soon offer will write. I am

Dʳ Sir

Your most obedient and

obliged humˡᵉ Serᵗ   GPaton

Customhouse Edinburgh
   21 Novemʳ 1772

Address: To The Reverend Dʳ Thomas Percy
         Easton Maudit
           near Castle Ashby Northamptonshire
             [*Enclosure* ¹¹]

Borrowed from the faculty of Advocates their library by me A. B.—Bannantyne's MS. Poems Gifted to the Advocates Lib. by the Earl of Hyndford. To be returned in six months from the Date of the Recepit.

London   Decʳ 1772

to be signed

A.B.

XXXV

From Paton¹

[December 31, 1772]

Dear Sir

Some time ago I wrote you agreeable to your Direction, which hope reached you how soon the Volume of Songs are put into my

¹¹ British Museum, Add. MS. 32332, f. 37. This draft receipt was evidently sent to Percy as a specimen of the kind of receipt that he was to make out. See his own receipt, p. 56. (The draft receipt, in a hand resembling that of the librarian, Alexander Brown, may have been enclosed in this letter or perhaps in another letter now missing.)

¹ *Source:* Harvard College Library, bMS Eng 893 (9E).

Hands it shall be transmitted to you to be left at His Grace of Northumberland's House in London.

You will please excuse my not writing you sooner as intended after seing in Mr Davidson's Hands the old Song or Poem *Peblis to the Play*, to which are annexed many very just and necessary explanatory Notes, if you think these few hints worth your while in order to elucidate the Poem these are at your Service. I shall be extremely happy that you oblige the World in publishing it or any things else are saved from Oblivion thro' your carefull kind Hand.

I am still of the Opinion that this Poem is a Composition of Sir David Lindsay Lyon King at Arms as the Scene is in the County where he lived and not far distant from his Country Seat the *Mount* near Skirling a small Town in that same County; this Song probably has taken Rise from some Rural Amusements occasioned or shewn at the *Annual Mercat* or *Fair* as termed here, which to this Time is yearly held at Peebles the chief Town of the County of *Tweedale*

[p. 2.] or *Peebles*, this Fair is now kept about the | Middle of May, and must justly be termed *Beltane* Fair, for a Discription of the Country Ceremonies of that Season of the Year please take *Pennant's* [2] *Account* 1st Edition page 90 and 91 in his *Tour in Scotland Year 1769.* these Rites are still observed in many Places of Scotland yet. That Sir David was an eminent Writer in James V. is unquestionable: however shall acknowledge myself justly corrected to be taught by you, who the real Author may be: of which be pleased to instruct me: if I can meet with any old Scotish almanack to fix the precise Day of this *Fair* if different from the Period now being the 2^d Wednesday of May, of this you shall have Notice soon, but you will observe it is not very far distant from *Beltane* [3] a Pastoral Rite used by our *Sheep &^{o} Herds* and this County of Peebles is remarkable for breeding *Cattle, Sheep &^{o}* and not much Tillage, these Diversions might have been kept on a *Green* or ffeild of Grass hard by the Town, and where Pedlars erect their Tents for vending their Wares &^{c}

[2] Thomas Pennant (1726–98), traveler and naturalist, *A Tour in Scotland*, Chester, 1771.
[3] The Beltane festival was celebrated on the first of May. It was also one of the four quarter days, the others being Hallowmas, Candlemas, and Lammas.

Stanza 2

Reeling [4]—The Women anxious to get as long Time as possible to amuse themselves, rose early in the Morning and occupied themselves in *reeling their Yarn into Hanks,* either of Flax or Wool

3

Gend—probably giddy or glad, fond of Diversion

5

Hopcalzie & *Cardronna*—these are two Gentlemen's Seats in this County *Cailzie* & Hopcalzie or High Calzie. Hop used often for a Mountain or raising Ground

6

Birkin Hat—I am at a Loss how to understand this, as I cannot fix the Time when *Hats* instead of *Bonnets* were first worn in | this [p. 3.] Country or whether any such Wear was used in Scotland as Hats woven of *Birch Twigs* as the moderns of *Straw.* Q. whether may it not be *Barkin'd* or stain'd with Greese and Dust; it is an usual expression amongst the Vulgar.—Bonnets were & are yet the common rural Covering for the Heads of Men.

7

Cleikit—hastily or quickly begun a rough Song.—this Word is different from *kekill* in Stanza 22. of which afterwards

8

Malkin—or Makin a Country rustic Word used For the female Secret Parts.
Our gude—too good.

11

Laugh. [5]—a very common Expression in Scotland used when any Company or Person receiving a Treat at a Tavern or Alehouse those

---

[4] *Reeling,* or *reilling* as in the MS. (pronunciation of the two spellings is identical), means *stir* or *confusion.*

[5] *Laugh* or *lauche* means *reckoning.*

who were treated, Say, *you will take my, or, our, Laugh in* or Treat again.

12

Trencheur—alluding to the usual common method in Scotland of collecting the Money from each Person at Marriage Feasts &ᶜ *Shuite* ⁶ *ane Dunt*—Q. *If not should have an Dunt or Stroke of me.*

14

Thirtie Sum—used in numbering Sheep *a Sum* or *Soume* is one Sheep, this term is constantly said in all *Sheep pasturage Counties in Scotland.* & Law Papers, or Rights to Lairds places are discribed to pasture such a Number of *Soums* of Sheep.

15

N.B. There appear to be wanting two Lines in this Stanza.
Styme—undistinct Vision or Sight, generally said when a Person's Eyes are filled with flying Dust from the High Way &ᶜ *or Stour* as exprest in this Country, so that no object can be scarcely seen.

17

anis—once

18

I wait—I know well, what it was: My own gray Mare threw me off *forfochtin faynt*—overcome, much fatigued, faint

19

[p. 4.] *The Stringis &ᶜ*—certainly alludes to some old Proverbial Expression, but do not remember it.
Sewin Sum—Seven Persons as in Stanza 14.

---

⁶ *Shuite* is a misreading for *service* meaning "deserves" or "deservest."

20

hockit—discribing the manner of dancing both in Highlands & Low Country of Scotland—at any Merriment or Festivity the common Dance is *Reels,* moving more slowly as the Tune invites, then footing quickly as the same directs, at this Time the Man to shew his alert ability raises first one then his other Leg & clapps the Palms of his Hands with a Noise below his *Hoch* or *Ham:* this excites great Mirth to the Spectators: so *this large clumsey Miller* is well discribed to *have hock it heavylie,* reel'd or danced dully.

that Tyd—that Time.

22

Seekill [7]—This *Tibby* appears to have come from the Miln hard by which there is commonly a small *hill,* or rising Ground composed of the Chaff or Husk of Oats, after the Grain is *kiln dried* before it can be grinded down into Meal. this Operation is often done by the Females so that *Tiby* may be his Maid, Mistress or Wife

kekill—laugh, this is usually applied to a Hen when she makes a Noise before Laying or dropping an Egg, and frequently discriptive of a person laughing

26

Q. If this Stanza is defective as N° 15.

With the felicitations of the Season I am

Dr Sir

Your most obedient humble

Servant   G Paton

Customhouse Edinburgh
  31 Decem^r 1772.

[7] A mistake for *heckill,* a form of *heckle.*

XXXVI
From Percy[1]

London, Jany. 9th 1773.

Dear Sir,

I received the very obliging favour of your last and thank you for
the trouble you were so good as to take in illustrating the old Poem
of Peebles to the Play: Many of the Notes are quite new to me, yet
very ingenious. If I am inclined to differ from you in opinion, it is
with regard to the Author and date of the Poem above mentioned:
I do not see the least resemblance between the Style of this old Song

[p. 2.] and the Compositions of Sr David Lindsay: and it surely | bears all
the Marks of an earlier Period. The language and idiom more an-
cient, more rustic, more native Scotch. But I shall reserve this Subject for a further Discussion,[2] and at present write [3] a few Lines
merely to express my acknowledgements for all your obliging favours.

Whenever you have a convenient opportunity to forward the Collection of Scottish Songs to me, I shall be extremely glad to see them:
but would not have you give yourself too much trouble as to the time

[p. 3.] when. Indeed, Mr John Davidson | (one of the Clerks of the
Signet) is to send me up a Manuscript of which Lord Hyndford has
procured me the Loan out of the Advocates Library. It will be sufficient if the Songs, or anything which you may have to send me,
come along with that MS.

Believe me to be

Dear Sir
Your obliged and
Most obedient Servant
Thos Percy

---

[1] *Source:* National Library of Scotland, MS. 29-5-8, Vol. I, f. 65;
printed in Maidment, pp. 19–20.

[2] See Letter XL, p. 57.
[3] MS. reads "wrote."

XXXVII
From Paton[1]

[February 26, 1773]

Dear Sir

By a Friend going to Sea yesterday I send you Pitscottie's History of Scotland fol. and Ferguson's Poems[2] these will be left for you at Northumberland House soon after the Arrival of the Ship at London.

You may please look into Macpherson's Dissertations[3] and Macpherson's Introduction to the History of Britain,[4] where you will find sufficient discussions about *Beltane*.[5]

I find that the Meaning of the Word *Soum* or *Sum*[6] when applied to Sheep, Oxen &c[a] varies as to Number in different Counties in

[1] *Source:* British Museum, **Add. MS.** 32332, f. 38.

[2] *Poems by Robert Fergusson*, Edinburgh, 1773, 12°, printed by Walter and Thomas Ruddiman. A volume preserved in the library of the University of St. Andrews (PR 3448 F3 D73) contains (a) *Poems* (1773) inscribed on the flyleaf in the poet's hand "To M[r] David Herd as a small mark of Esteem & Friendship from his much obliged humble Serv[t] R Fergusson"; (b) *Poems on Various Subjects, By Robert Fergusson*, Part II, Edinburgh, 1779, 12°; (c) a MS. list of "Poems wrote by Robert Fergusson after the publication of his Works"; (d) a newspaper cutting of a poem "When teased with vapours . . . ," described as previously unpublished.

[3] John Macpherson, D.D. (1713–65), minister of Sleat, Isle of Skye, *Critical Dissertations on the Origin, Antiquities, Language . . . of the Ancient Caledonians*, London, 1768, 4°. It has no direct reference to the Beltane ceremony.

[4] James Macpherson (1736–96), "Ossian." *An Introduction to the History of Great Britain and Ireland*, 1771, 4°, p. 164; third edition, 1773, 4°, pp. 221–24.

[5] "Beltane" occurs in the opening line of *Peblis to the Play*, "At beltane quhen ilk bodie bownis."

[6] "soum," "sum," "sowme"—the proportion of cattle or sheep to pasture; "a soum of grass"—as much as will pasture one cow or five sheep.

Scotland and often used as discriptive of the Quantity of Pasturage and for Grazing Cattle or Sheep in Charters.

Since you do not expect the M.SS. Collection of Scot's Poems by Bannantyne so soon, I hope to have the Opportunity shortly of looking it over and if by any Means I can make complete my Copy of S. David Lindesay's Satyres,[7] of which will write you, as I am persuaded there are many of his Poems in that Collection.

Lately was discovered in the Advocates' Liberary one or two Poems [8] printed about the Time of the Reformation, the Titles of which will inform of after inquiry has been made about the Authors, these relate to the Reformation, and certainly have been overlookt by the Collector of the Catalogue in making it up, as these are short and make a thin Volume [9] of Pamphlets. I am

Dear Sir

Your most obedient Servant

GPaton

Customhouse Edinburgh
    26 February 1773

Address: To The Reverend Dr Thomas Percy
            Northumberland House

Docket: Mr Paton
        1773

[7] See Letter XLII, n. 2, p. 61.
[8] Probably some of the *Sempill*

Ballates. See edition by T. G. Stevenson, Edinburgh, 1872, 8°.
[9] Over "Book" deleted.

XXXVIII
From Paton[1]

[April 24, 1773]

Dear Sir

Some Days ago M[r] Davidson informed me that you wanted a Copy of *E. Surry's poetical Version of the Ecclesiastes*,[2] after which I have been ever since making Search to no manner of purpose, as it is not to be found in any Shop here, nor in any of our publick Liberaries; but if you could specifie more particularly the[3] Title I would pursue a further Inquiry, please inform of the Earl's Surname. Is it Howard? of the Arundell Family; in looking slightly into M[r] West's Catalogue[4] of rare Books I do not meet with it there.

I hope you got Pitscottie's History, which caused leave for you at Northumberland house London: in a few Weeks will transmit you a small Tract on our Highland Clans[5] printed some Years ago but never published of late.

Please to let me know if I can be of any Service to you here and shall chearfully obey your Orders to the utmost of my power, being
D[r] Sir
Your most obliged and obedient
humble Serv[t]   GPaton

[1] *Source:* British Museum, Add. MS. 32332, f. 40.
[2] See Letter XL, p. 57. Percy had advertised for this as early as 1763, and it was not till about 1775 that he found it among the MSS. of Henry Harington, D.D. (1755–91). See *The Correspondence of Thomas Percy and Richard Farmer*, ed. Cleanth Brooks, Baton Rouge, 1946, pp. 47–48 and Appendix.
[3] MS. reads "the the."

[4] The *Catalogue of the . . . Library of James West* (1704?–72), President of the Royal Society. His collection was notably rich in the older English poetry. The sale commenced 29 March 1773.
[5] *The History of the Feuds and Conflicts Among the Clans*, Glasgow, 1764, reprinted in *Miscellanea Scotica*, Glasgow, 1818, I, No. III. See Letter XLI, p. 59.

Customhouse Edinburgh
24 April 1773

PS. If you now desire *"Le Grys* Translation of *V. Paterculus"* [6] 12°
it shall be at your Service as I've pickt up a Copy lately.

Address: To The Reverend Dr Thomas Percy
Northumberland house
London

XXXIX

From Percy[1]

[This letter of *c.* April 27, 1773 is missing.]

[*Enclosure*[2]]

Northumberland House, London
27th Day of April 1773
This day is borrowed by me Thomas Percy, out of the Library
belonging to the Faculty of Advocates at Edinburgh, a MS. Collection of Poems (writ by George Banantyne and lately presented to
the said Library by the Earl of Hyndford) to be returned in Six
Months. Witness my hand

Thomas Percy

Docket: Mr Percy's
Receipt for
Bannantyne's
MS. Poems

---

[6] See Letter XVIII, n. 3, p. 27.
[1] Presumably there was a letter in
which the receipt was enclosed.
[2] *Source:* British Museum, Add.
MS. 32332, f. 42. This was posted

before Percy received the MS., which
left Edinburgh on 7 May (see Letter
XLI, p. 59) and was acknowledged
3 June 1773 (see Letter XLII, p. 61).

XL

From Percy[1]

London, May 1. 1773

Dear Sir,

Nothing but the very alarming illness of one of my Children [2] (who is thank God happily recovered) could have prevented me from acknowledging your many obliging favours so long. Pittiscottie's History is come safe to hand, and is extremely acceptable.

The Paterculus you mention I do not want; and the little book of the Conflicts of the Clans [3] (if that is what you mean in your last) I have had some years, but my Copy has no Preface, &c: and is printed at Glasgow 1764. If any Preface &c has been added since that time I should be glad to see it.

—The Version of Ecclesiastes in English Verse [4] was made by Henry Howard Earl of Surrey,[5] son and father to two successive Dukes of Norfolk. | You will find an account of him and his poetical [p. 2.] Works in the 1st Vol. of Mr Walpole's Royal and Noble Authors, 8vo and in the 1st Vol. of Athenæ Oxonienses by A. Wood [6] fol°—I am going to publish this Lord Surrey's Poems,[7] and shall beg your acceptance of a Copy: but I can no where recover this Poetical Translation of Ecclesiastes: it does not exist in any of our public Libraries; nor could I ever get sight of it in any catalogue for sale.

I have made a great Discovery. I have found out that the old

---

[1] *Source:* National Library of Scotland, MS. 29-5-8, Vol. I, f. 66; printed in Maidment, pp. 20–23.

[2] Henry Percy (1763–83), at this time King's Scholar at Westminster. He became ill on 27 March (see Percy's *Journal*).

[3] See Letter XXXVIII, p. 55.

[4] See Letter XXXVIII, n. 2, p. 55.

[5] Born in 1517; beheaded in 1547. His father was Thomas, the third Duke of Norfolk; his son was Thomas, the fourth Duke.

[6] Anthony Wood (1632–95), the Oxford antiquary.

[7] For the history of this uncompleted edition, see Percy-Farmer *Correspondence*, pp. 175–200.

Poem of *Peebles to the Play,* was the Composition of King James 1ˢᵗ of Scotland.[8] I am indebted to John Major's [9] History de *Gestis* [p. 3.] *Scotorum* for this curious piece of Intelligence. See Lib. VI. cap. 14.—His words are "Composuit . . . artificiosam cantilenam . . . "*Yas Sen* [10] *&c.* et jucundum artificiosumque illum cantum; *at* "*Beltayn &c* quem alij de Dalkeith et Gargeil, mutare studuerunt "quia in arce aut camera clausus servabatur, in qua mulier cum "matre habitabat."

There can be no doubt but the jucund and artificial Song, *at Beltayne* &c. is the old Poem of *Peebles to the Play,* as it begins with this Line

At Beltayne, quhen ilk bodie boūdis

To Peebles to the Play

but the rest of Major's words are to me perfectly unintelligible; as the first words of the other Song he quotes are apparently corrupted. [p. 4.] viz. *Yas sen &c* | I wish you would examine the Passages in Major's Book and compare it in different Editions: as also show it to some ingenious antiquaries; particularly my good friend Mʳ Davidson Clerk of the Signet to whom my best Respects. Be pleased to tell him that I now hope to receive the old MS. Collection of Poems which was formerly Lord Hyndford's. At the end of this Month or beginning of the next I shall leave London for the Summer and consequently,

---

[8] Percy also discusses this in the Percy-Hailes *Correspondence,* pp. 128, 129–30. James I's authorship is disputed by Skeat in *The Kingis Quair* (1884), pp. xix–xxi, but a strong counterargument is advanced by T. F. Henderson in *Scottish Vernacular Literature,* third edition, Edinburgh, 1910, pp. 103–12.

[9] John Major or Mair (1469–1550), historian and scholastic divine, professor of philosophy and divinity in the University of Glasgow and Provost of St. Salvator's College in the University of St. Andrews, *His-* *toria Maioris Britanniæ,* Paris, 1521, 4°; Edinburgh, 1740, 4°. The passage is identical in the Paris and Edinburgh editions and plainly refers to the romantic way in which James I, King of Scots, met his future queen in the castle where he was held captive by Henry IV.

[10] "Yas Sen" is probably a corruption of "Sen that eyne," the opening words of the "Sang on absence" printed in Pinkerton's *Ancient Scotish Poems,* 1786, II, 214. But see Henderson, *Scottish Vernacular Literature,* p. 103.

if the Book should come after that time I shall not see it for many
Months, not to mention the Danger it will run of being lost.

I am

Dear Sir

Your obliged humble Servant

Tho. Percy

XLI

From Paton[1]

[May 7, 1773]

Dear Sir

Ever since I wrote you have been upon the Search for the Version
of Ecclesiastes to no purpose. The Tract on the Conflicts of the
Clans altho' printed in 1764 was not published till my Inquiry lately
for it to transmit to Mr Pennant,[2] how Messrs Foulis delay'd it so
long is beyond my Comprehension, there is no Preface &^c to it, you
may command a Copy at pleasure.

I shall examine the Passage of John Major and compare the two
Editions of the Book as there are no more than one printed at Paris
by Bad. Ascensius and Freebairn's Edinburgh one 4to from the later
of which you make the Extract, of which in a Post or two for I have
not the Paris Edition by me at the time.

Mr Davidson read yours to me offers his Compliments and writes
you soon, he that Day put into my hands *Bannantine's* [3] *M.SS. Collection of Poems*, which I this day packt up in a Box covered with an
Oil painted Cloth addrest for you at Northumberland house London, which is already gone from Edinburgh on it's way to you:—in

---

[1] *Source:* British Museum, Add.
MS. 32332, f. 43.
[2] See Letter XXXV, n. 2, p. 48.
[3] There are many forms of the
name Bannatyne in sixteenth-century
documents: *The Bannatyne Manuscript*, ed. Ritchie, I, xxxiv–v.

the same Box you will find Sir David Lindsay's Satyres of which I
[p. 2.] wrote you formerly, from the slight View I have had of | Bannan-
tyne's M.SS. I am in great Hopes to recover what the printed Copy
wants,[4] as I think these Interludes are contained in it, so have used
the freedom of sending you a Sight of that exceeding scarce Book of
Sir David Lindsay, no where can I hear of another Copy: for I do
not think that very scarce piece of his in the Bodleian Liberary is or
can be the same with this Book, vide Bod. Catalogue under Lyndesay
of the Mount.—it's the old Edition of the Catalogue [5] I have in one
Vol fol—I hope the Box will reach you before your quitting London
as it comes by the Waggon.

Excuse the freedom used in my putting under your Cover this
Letter for Mr Gough, who will be exceeding fond of viewing
Bannantyne's M.S.S. indulge him also with a Sight of Sir David
Lindsay's Satyres: he will send for the small parcel addrest to him in
the Box; of which the inclosed advises him.

I delivered your Letters. Lord Hailes [6] is presently in the Country. I most sincerely congratulate you on the Recovery of your
Child [7] and am

Dear Sir
Your most obedient humble
Servt
GPaton

Customhouse Edinburgh
    7 May 1773

Address: To The Reverend Mr Thomas Percy
            Northumberland house
                London

---

[4] See Letters XXXVII, XLII, n. 2,
and XLIII, pp. 54, 61, and 62.
    [5] *Catalogus Impressorum Librorum
in Bibliotheca Bodlejana*, Oxford,
1674, folio. The Bodleian catalogue
of 1738 is in two volumes.
    [6] Percy had written to Lord Hailes

on 1 May and perhaps had asked
Paton to deliver the letter. See also
the postscript of Letter XLIII, p. 62.
    [7] Henry, who as Percy's *Journal*
shows, had been ill during much of
March and April.

XLII
From Percy [1]

London, June 3ᵈ 1773

Dear Sir,

I have just received the parcel you have been so good as to send me, containing *Bannatine's MS; Sʳ David Lindsay's Satires*—and the Packet for Mʳ Gough; which shall be most carefully delivered to him.—I have but just peeped into the MS. and into Lindsay's Satires:—I see plainly that the MS. contains a compleat Copy of the Satires; [2] but somewhat different from the printed Edition.—In the Course of the Summer, I shall examine both with due attention, and shall inform you of the result. Mʳ Gough was with me when I received the Letter you had inclosed for him, which I presented to him.—When you meet with the Paris Edition of *Joh. Major's History* I will be obliged to you if you will note the variations in the Passage of pag.309. (Edit.Edimburgi. 1740:) and favour | me with them. [3] [p. 2.] In one of your former Letters you mention your being possessed of "Le Grys Translation of V. Paterculus 12º." I shall be much obliged to you for a Transcript [4] of the Title-page: and remain with a due sense of your many kind repeated favours

Dear Sir
Your much obliged
humble Servant
Tho. Percy

[1] *Source:* National Library of Scotland, MS. 29-5-8, Vol. I, f. 67; printed in Maidment, pp. 23–24.
[2] The Bannatyne MS. version is not complete. See Lindsay's *Works*, ed. D. Hamer (Scottish Text Society), Edinburgh, 1936, IV, 134–35. Volume II prints parallel texts of the version of 1552, preserved in the Bannatyne MS., and that of 1554 published in the Charteris quarto edition of 1602.
[3] See Letter XLIII, p. 62.
[4] Over "Copy" deleted.

XLIII
From Paton[1]

Customhouse Edinburgh 7 June 1773

Dear Sir

I am happy the Parcel has at last reached you, will be pleased in your finding Entertainment with *Bañantine's Collection* and that your views of compleating Sir David Lindsay's Satyres are so certain, the Summer Season will perfect your Expectations: in these Inquiries I wish your Health and Pleasure to accomplish your design.

From The [1a] slight view I had of the Paris Edition of *John Major's History*, corresponds with the Edin[r] Edition 1740 but shall I hope in my next[2] give you a transcript from it, with a Translation attended with some historical critical notes if I once had time to collect the opinions of some few Acquaintances, as I must confess the *Passage in this Author* is obscure to me, but of this afterwards.

As you desire I have subjoined the Title page of "Le Grys Translation of V. Paterculus[3] 12° " but you are welcome to the Book on a Call.

Forgive the Freedom of my inclosing a Letter for M[r] Gough, am solicitous for his Answer, if favourable, I shall beg your Acceptance of a publication (I write him of) how soon it is done, as a small testimony of the many marks of your Friendship conferr'd on
> D[r] Sir
> Your most obedient and obliged humble Servant
> GPaton

P.S. all your Letters shall be most carefully delivered as addrest but all the Gentlemen are in the Country.   GP

---

[1] *Source:* British Museum, Add. MS. 32332, ff. 45–46.
[1a] Paton forgot to delete "From."

[2] No letter with this transcript has been traced. See Letter XL, n. 9, p. 58.
[3] See Letter XXXVIII, p. 56.

[*Enclosure*]

Velleius Paterculus
His
Romane
Historie:

In two Bookes.

Exactly translated out of
the Latine Edition super-
vised by Inus Gruterus.
According to the reformations in
such parts of him, in which the Latin
hath suffered either by time, or negli-
gence in the transcribers of the ablest
Commentars upon him.

and renderd English
By
Sir Robert Le Grys K^{nt}

London
Printed by M.F. for R. Swaine,
in Britaines-Burse at the Signe of the
Bible MDCXXXII

XLIV

From Paton[1]

[This letter of June–July 1773 is missing.]

[1] Implied in Letter XLIII.

XLV

From Percy[1]

Alnwick Castle, Aug.20.1773.

Dear Sir,

Since I had the pleasure of seeing you at Edinburgh,[2] I have been reading Mr Pennant's *Tour thro' Scotland*.[3] 8vo and in pag. 92. of his 2^d Edit. 1772, he speaks of a Scotch Poet, whom I never before heard of, viz. Robertson of Struan,[4] who had been in the Rebellions of 1715 and 1745, and who (he says) left behind him a Volume of Elegies and other Pieces.—I should be glad if you could inform me when and where they were printed, and what degree of merit they have: if worth buying, I should be glad if you would [p. 2.] procure me the Volume | The price of which I shall with thanks repay you: Being with great regard

Dear Sir

Your very faithful

Humble Servant

Thos Percy

PS/

I hope you have performed your obliging Promise in making excuses for my not being able to visit my Friends in and about Edinburgh in consequence of my short stay. From Edinburgh I went to Inverary, and got back to Alnwick Castle by Saturday night.[5]

---

[1] *Source:* National Library of Scotland, MS. 29-5-8, Vol. I, f. 68; printed in Maidment, pp. 24–26.

[2] Percy's *Journal*, 9 August 1773, reads: "I visited Mr Boswell, Mr Davidson and Mr Paton."

[3] See Letter XXXV, n. 2, p. 48.

[4] Alexander Robertson (1670–

1749), thirteenth Baron of Struan, *Poems On Various Subjects and Occasions*, Edinburgh, 1751, 8°.

[5] Percy's visit had not been planned beforehand, and though he was in Scotland from 8 to 14 August, he was in Edinburgh for only a fraction of that time. The relevant entries

XLVI
From Paton[1]

[August 23, 1773]

Dear Sir

I am favoured with yours of 20th Current, wrote the Cards of Apology for your not waiting on [1a] your Acquaintances, Dr. Blair told me he design'd to write you which hope he has done. My Lord Hailes I know has ordered you a Copy of his late Publication on the Scotish History,[2] else I should have transmitted one, it will be delivered at London I suppose by M[r] Caddell.[3]

You may look for *Struan Robertson's Poems* by the Newcastle Carrier or Waggon this or next Week, their Merit is not very eminent, tho' now scarce but will provide you, alongst therewith you shall have the Translation of *M[r] Ruddiman's Preface* to Andersoni Diplom. and Numismata Scotia,[4] this is a Composition most accurately

in his *Journal* read: "[7 August] M[r] Durant called on me, accompanied with M[r] and Miss Beaufoy. . . . M[r] D. then requested me to go with them to Edinburgh. We set out in the evening . . . . got to Edinburgh before it was dark. . . . Sunday August 8th In the Evening, at the chief Episcopal Chapel . . . I married George Durant Esq of Tong Castle in Shropshire Member of Parliament for Evesham, to Miss Maria Beaufoy. . . . [9 August] I visited M[r] Boswell and M[r] Davidson and M[r] Paton. [10 August] Br[eakfast] with M[r] Boswell and went with him to the Court of Sessions &c. About 2 o'clock we set out on a Tour to Inverary. . . . Got to Glasgow in the evening—[11 August] Walked about the town of Glasgow. . . . [12 August] Went to

Inverary to breakfast. . . . [13 August] . . . returned to Glasgow to dinner: then proceeded back to Edinburgh and got there in very good time: took my leave of M[r] and M[rs] Durant, set out at 4 o'clock in the Newcastle Post Coach. . . . [14 August] Br[eakfast] near Lauder . . . Tea at Whittingham, home [at Alnwick]."

[1] *Source:* British Museum, Add. MS. 32332, f. 47.

[1a] MS. reads "of."

[2] *Remarks on the History of Scotland. By Sir David Dalrymple, Edinburgh,* 1773, 12°.

[3] Thomas Cadell (1742–1802), bookseller and publisher in London.

[4] See Letter XXV, n. 4, p. 36. *An Introduction to Mr James Anderson's Diplomata Scotiæ* . . . , by Thomas

done but the Translator has not done Justice to so valuable a performance it must be productive of a better one afterwards, wish some
eminent hand would oblige the World with it and set of Plates of the
Coins adding what has been discovered since this last, your short
stay in Town I forgot to send to your Lodgings, as also to get the 2ᵈ
Volume of the Scot's Songs, but if you remain any Time at Alnwick
Castle I will endeavour to procure it's transmission that you may look
it over, the Collector will be fond of your Opinion.

[p. 2.]   I should be glad to know, who purchased the 3 Vol. fol. of the
old Ballats, p. 124 Nº 2112 fol. or if intended to be republished, these
sold at a very high rate in Mʳ West's Auction.⁵ Amongst same Collection there was a 4ᵗᵒ entitled the *Three Tales by the Priestes of
Peebles,*⁶ I thought this had been commissioned by the Advocates
here, but was not, the Catalogue is not presently in my Possession
but will note the Number and page in my next to you.

If you can be indulged a longer Space for perusing the M.S.S.
shall talk to Mʳ Davidson if possible to get it prolonged, so that you
may enjoy full time to make your Notes &ᶜ. I ever am

Dear Sir

Your much obliged and obedᵗ

humble Servant   GPaton

Customhouse Edinburgh

23 August 1773

Ruddiman, M.A., Edinburgh, 1773, 8º.

⁵ See Letter XXXVIII, n. 4, p. 55. The sale of his library went on for twenty-four days, March and April, 1773. Lot 2112 is described in the Catalogue as "*A Curious Collection of old Ballads, in Number above* 1200, b.l. *with humorous Frontis-pieces,* 3 vol." It was purchased by Thomas Pearson for £20. See Letter XLVIII, n. 4, p. 69.

⁶ *The thrie Tailes of the thrie Priests of Peblis. . . . Imprinted at*

Edinburgh be Robert Charteris, 1603, 4º. See edition by T. D. Robb (Scottish Text Society), Edinburgh, 1920. The Introduction, p. vii, incorrectly states that the "sole survivor" of the Charteris edition of 1603 is the Bodleian Library copy (Douce R. 527). There is one in the National Library of Scotland (Ry. II.f.21), and another is mentioned in Rosenbach's catalogue of *English Poetry to 1700* (1941), Lot 56. The author is unknown.

PS. Since writing the above the Catalogue has been returned to me. p. 109. Quarto N° 1820. "*The thrie Tailes of the thrie Priestes of Peblis B.l. impr. at Edinb^r be Rob. Charteris 1603.*" is it possible to trace out the Purchaser? ⁷

Mr Boswell told me he had seen you after your Return from Inverary.

Address: To The Reverend Dr Thomas Percy
      Alnwick Castle

XLVII
From Paton¹

[September 7, 1773]

Revd Dear Sir

I hope by this Time you have received the small Parcel from the Newcastle Carrier as I wrote you formerly.

Having seen the Collector of the *Scot's Songs*,² last day he declined sending you the materials for a Second Volume as these already inserted in the Volume have too much of Novelty, very imperfect &^c that he would seem to have dropt his intention of publishing any more at this time unless his Success is more engaging afterwards in picking up Materials.

I mentioned to Mr Davidson my Proposal of your having a prolonged Time of keeping the Manuscript Poems, from the Advocates Liberary, which he did not think would be refused, so desired me to suggest Your writing a Letter to Mr Brown ³ Librarian to the Faculty requesting some more Months allowance for perusing it, which he might communicate to the Faculty Curators at their first

---

⁷ John Ratcliffe (d. 1776), the collector, whose library was sold by auction 27 March 1776.

¹ *Source:* British Museum, Add. MS. 32332, f. 49.

² See Letter XII, n. 5, p. 22.

³ Alexander Brown (d. 1801), librarian to the Faculty of Advocates, 1776–94.

Meeting, and make no doubt of it's being granted and will make
[p. 2.] you enjoy it all Winter; nothing shall be wanting on | my part to
promote this Indulgence, and sure I am Mr Brown the Librarian
will not oppose your or my Request, if you transmit the Letter to
me I will deliver it, and importune a Consent.

Please let me know if you want any other article from this 'ere
you push Southward. I ever am

Dear Sir
Your obliged and most obed^t
humble Servt   GPaton

Customhouse Edinburgh
    7 Septem^r 1773

Address: To The Reverend Dr Thomas Percy   Alnwick Castle

XLVIII

From Percy[1]

Alnwick Castle, Sep^m 11.1773

Dear Sir,

I only deferred thanking you for your very obliging Letter, till I
could inform you of my having safely received the Packet you were
so good as to send, containing *Struan's Poems* and the *Translation* of
the Preface to Anderson's Diplom. &c. I received them safe today
and am much obliged to you for so kindly procuring them for me:
but must beg you to let me repay you the cost, otherwise I shall be
affraid to mention my literary wants to you another time.—You have
already laid me under so many obligations by your former[2] obliging
presents, that I am ashamed to trespass still further on your good-

---

[1] *Source:* National Library of Scot-   printed in Maidment, pp. 26–31,
land, MS. 29-5-8, Vol. I, f. 69;   where it is misdated September 19.
                            [2] Over "for" deleted.

nature:—nor shall I rest till I obtain a present of an Houshold Book for you, as a small pledge of friendship.

I should be very glad to peruse the 2ᵈ Vol. of Scots Songs in MS.— [p. 2.] but the transmission to this place is so uncertain by the Waggon which I apprehend does not come through this Town, that I am affraid to let you hazzard it: If you thought you could venture it to London, I would look it over at my leisure and return it towards Spring; or ³ when I send back the Ancient MS.

The 3 volˢ of Old Ballads, which were in Mʳ West's Sale, were bought by a friend of mine, Major Pearson: ⁴ they consisted of loose detached ballads collected into Volˢ—Such as are still sold on stalls; not one in a hundred of them fit to be republished; and the best among them, were the same as what I had selected out of Pepys's Collection ⁵ for | my former Publication.—I did not take notice of [p. 3.] the 4ᵗᵒ piece which you inquire after (viz. *The 3 Talis by the Priestis of Peblis*) during the time of the sale; but in the course of the ensuing Winter, I will make it my business to inquire who purchased it, and give you information on that head.

I am extremely obliged to you for being so kind as to send circular excuses to my friends for not calling on them during my very short stay in Edinburgh.——

After I left you, Mʳ Durant prevailed on me to accompany him in a Tour to Inverary ⁶ in which we were exceedingly amused indeed. But it took up all my short time in Scotland: for I did not return to Edinburgh till 10 o'clock on Friday night and I set off for Alnwick at 4 o'clock on Saturday Morning.— | It was after Mʳ Boswell was [p. 4.] gone to bed on Friday night that I called at his Door.⁷

³ After "but this" deleted.
⁴ This collection was formed by Robert Harley, first Earl of Oxford. On the dispersal of the Harleian Library, it was acquired by James West and, on his death, was purchased in April 1773 by Thomas Pearson (1740?–81), Major on the Bengal establishment. When Pearson's books were sold in 1788, the collection was acquired by the Duke of Roxburghe, and came to be known as the Roxburghe Ballads. It has been in the British Museum since 1845.
⁵ In Magdalene College, Cambridge.
⁶ See Letter XLV, n. 5, pp. 64–65.
⁷ See Postscript of Letter XLV, p. 64.

You are so good as to say you will try to get my time for keeping the old MS. extended: it would be extremely acceptable indeed. But I fear the application will be without success.—You may however hint my wishes on that head to my good friend Mr John Davidson:—to whom my kindest Respects: at the same time tell him his old acquaintance Mr Collingwood Foster [8] of this Town would be much obliged to him, if he could procure him the last and best folio Edition of *Forduni Scoti Chronicon:* he forgot to mention it when he wrote to him lately.—I am   Dear Sir

Your most obliged Servant
Tho. Percy

XLIX

From Paton[1]

[September 16, 1773]

Dear Sir

Some days ago I received yours of 11th Current. am glad that the Parcel has reached you, since the Conveyance by the Waggon to Newcastle is precarious shall omit sending you any thing that way unless you expressly desire otherways, during your Stay at Alnwick Castle: but shall probably have Occasion of transmitting some things to London this Winter, when I will endeavour to procure this volume of the *Scots' Songs* as it is and to be put into your Hands, till then delay writing any further on that Subject

I am glad you enjoyed such an agreeable Excursion altho' rapid, that Tour is entertaining, engaging Prospects open with Variety amongst these northern Hills.

---

[8] Collingwood Foster (1715–76), solicitor and Clerk of the Peace for Northumberland. See also "The Ancestry of Admiral Lord Collingwood," by J. C. Hodgson, in *Archæologia* *Aeliana. . . . Published by the Society of Antiquaries of Newcastle upon Tyne,* Third Series, II (1906), 154.

[1] *Source:* British Museum, Add. MS. 32332, ff. 51–52.

Mr John Davidson is presently in the Country but on his Return (which is lookt for soon) I shall communicate what you write me and you may assure Mr Collingwood Foster that it shall be my Study to join Mr Davidson's Search for *Forduni Scoti Chronicon,* which I hope to provide the Gentleman tho' unacquainted with yet shall be ready to serve him as your and Mr Davidson's Friend, and should he be very anxious of having it just now he shall be very welcome to the Use of my Copy till one is purchased for himself.

Accept of my Thanks for your kind Information about the Pur- [p. 2.] chaser of the *Old Ballads* and it's Contents. Major Pearson purchases Books in that Style &^c with great Avidity and Cost: so Mr Gough wrote me: he will certainly communicate to the World some things, that are of Value out of his great Collection.

I am sorry to give you the Trouble of inquiring about *The 3 Tales by the Priestis of Peblis,* but may be worthy looking into, whether it is a Performance of the Knight o' the Mount *Lindsay Sir David.*[2]

It were to be wisht that some accurate Gentleman would publish a complete Dictionary from Somner,[3] Spelman,[4] Bp. Kennet,[5] Chaucer,[6] Lydgate &c^a of our old Saxon and English Words; Lye's Junij Etymolog.[7] is not so extensive as I could wish: Mr Ruddiman merits

---

[2] See Letter XLVI, n. 6, p. 66.

[3] William Somner (1598–1699), *Dictionarium Saxonico-Latino-Anglicum,* Oxford, 1659, folio.

[4] Sir Henry Spelman (1564?–1641), *Henrici Spelmanni . . . Archæologus. In Modum Glossarii,* 1626, folio. See also *Glossarium Archaiologicum,* ed. Sir W. Dugdale, 1664, folio.

[5] White Kennet (1660–1728), Bishop of Peterborough, who published *Parochial Antiquities . . . with a Glossary of Obsolete Terms,* Oxford, 1695, 4°. *The Interpreter of Words and Terms. . . . First published by . . . Dr Cowel* [1554–1611] *. . . and continu'd by Tho. Manley. . . . Now further aug-* *mented and improv'd, by the addition of many thousand words,* 1701, folio, was also by Kennet. A copy with MS. notes by Bishop Tanner (1674–1735) is preserved in the Bodleian Library.

[6] Paton is presumably thinking of Thomas Speght's edition, 1598 and 1602, folio, with "old and obscure Words explaned," and of John Urry's edition, 1721, folio, ". . . with a Glossary."

[7] Edward Lye (1694–1767). From the MSS. of Franciscus Junius (1589–1677), he edited *F. Junii . . . Etymologicum Anglicanum,* Oxford, 1743, folio. Lye's *Dictionarium Saxonico et Gothico-Latinum* was completed after his death by Owen Manning, 1772, folio.

great Applause by his publication of Douglas's Virgil [8] but the Printer did him great Injustice in printing this valuable performance so wretchedly incorrect.

I observe in M[r] West's Catalogue N° 4593 *Essay Upon the Inscription of Macduff's Crosse in Fyfe* [9] *Edin[r] 1678 in 4[to]*, this was purchased (am told) for the Royal Liberary, to no purpose has been my Search for it here in all our public or private Liberaries, being a small Tract so has perished altho' the Title is preserved, yet I am apt to believe there are two Editions [10] of it, the latest one reprinted [p. 3.] in 4[to] Anno 1719 with other Tracts under this | Title *Miscellanea Scotica* [11] Vol I. N° 1 consisting of 57 pages the Explanation being only 17 pages, this I suppose is M[r] James Cuningham's but will not positively affirm it without comparing it with the one printed 1678. My Copy bears after the running Title of the Tract follows the Inscription for which please see *Sibbald's History of Fife and Kinross* [12] *p 93.* Then begins "Tho' I had this of an ingenious Gentleman, "telling me he came by it from the Clerk of Craill, (i.e. a Town in "Fife) who inform'd That several succeeding Clerks there, have, "for a considerable Time, engross'd this as a true Copy in their "Books, to preserve it from utter Perishing; for it is now quite worn "off the Stone, at least altogether illegible. But be it so recorded in "Craill" &c[a]. After this pretty long Introduction he proceeds to

[8] Ruddiman's glossary to Gavin Douglas's *Virgil's Æneis*, Edinburgh, 1710, folio. See Letter I, n. 8, p. 2.

[9] *An Essay Upon The Inscription of MACDUFF'S CROSSE IN FYFFE. by I.C. 1678. Edinburgh, Printed by the Heir of Andrew Anderson, Printer to the King's most Excellent Majesty*, 1678, 4°, 20 pp. I.C. is James Cunningham, Writer to the Signet.

[10] An edition with a drawing of the cross was published by William Adams, Edinburgh, 1716.

[11] *Miscellanea Scotica; being a Collection of the most curious Pieces relating to the Natural Ecclesiastical and Civil History of Scotland*, Edinburgh, 1719 (published by William Adams). Vol. I (of 57 pgs.) was the only one published. The work is rare. The *Essay* occupies pages 3–20, and the text does not differ substantially from that of the earlier editions. It was reprinted in *Scotia Rediviva: A Collection of Tracts Illustrative of the History and Antiquities of Scotland*, Edinburgh, 1826, pp. 257 ff. (also with different title, 1836).

[12] Sir Robert Sibbald (1641–1722), physician and antiquary, *The History, Ancient and Modern, of the Sheriffdoms of Fife and Kinross, Edinburgh M.D.CC.X.* folio. See pages 92–93.

explain every single word, deriving them from the Saxon &ᶜ making this Inscription intelligible, which by many is valued mere Gibberish, which could not be the original Intention of erecting a Cross and carving or engraving it on Stone.—If Convenience permit be pleased to look into His Grace of Northumberland's Liberary if Cuningham's own Edition of this Tract in 1678 be amongst the Valuable Collection, which you will easily know by comparing it with the first Sentence in my Book as above transcribed.—Was I once sure of this would cause reprint this Tract: you'l excuse my giving you this Trouble, having met with Silence from one of the Underlibrarians [13] to the King and expect no Satisfaction till Mʳ Gough returns to London this Winter, who in his obliging way will satisfie me if you are disappointed in not meeting with it in his Grace's Possession.

I transmitted yours to Dʳ Blair, who still remains at Leith.   [p. 4.]

Beg you will recall your Intention and still let me know, what you may want either for yourself or any Friend that I may enjoy the continued opportunities of expressing my Gratitude to you, for your Kindness, in the Literary way.

I shall use my utmost Care and Concern (if possible) to prevent the speedy recall of Banantine's M.S.S. and write of our Success. I am

> Revᵈ Dear Sir
> Your most obedient and obliged
> humble Servant   GPaton

Customhouse Edinburgh
    16 September 1773

PS. Mʳ Davidson having just now returned to Town, have concerted with him about *Forduni Scotici Chronicon* and the M.SS. of which afterwards. Receive the Inscription of a Ring [14] supposed to

---

[13] Probably Richard Graham mentioned in Letter VI, p. 15.

[14] The Ring of Alva is inscribed: ꞇ ᵹꞃ\\ ᶆꞃ\\ ᶓ\\ ꞃꞃ\\ ᶆ \\ᶓ\\ᶎ \\ ᶓ\\
Just below this inscription, on p. 131

of Add. MS. 32332, is pasted a printed slip which reads as follows: "Characters and figures upon a Gold Ring, dug up at Alva in the County of Stirling North Britain 1766, in have belonged to the Abbot of Cambuskenneth near Stirling: the Legend is not understood.

17 Septr 1773

L

From Percy[1]

Alnwick Castle, Octr 23.1773

Dear Sir,

I received your obliging favour of last Month but have been prevented from answering it before by a multiplicity of engagements. I shall be very glad to look over the Collection of Pieces provided for the 2^d Vol. of *Scots Songs*, at my leisure, if it can conveniently be spared.—Mr Forster of this Town will be much obliged to you & Mr Davidson for procuring him a Copy of the Folio Edition of *Scoti Chronicon of Fordun*, if such should fall in your way; but he is in no hurry about it and will be very well contented to await your [p. 2.] Leisure. At the same time he will be very thankful, if you | or Mr Davidson could procure him a Copy of Mr Foulis's fine folio Edition of Cæsar's Commentaries [2] in Latin, printed at Glasgow, to accompany *Fordun*.—

The Duke has no Edition of the *Essay on Macduff's Cross* &c. which you inquire after: Indeed his Grace's Library rather contains useful, than curious Books: He is not a Collector of things in our

---

clearing a field which had been coppice-wood past memory of man. The Diameter in the inside ⅝ inch. The weight 1 drop 27 grains. Fine Gold." (For "drop," an obsolete Scottish Troyweight, see O.E.D.)

[1] *Source:* National Library of Scot-

land, MS. 29-5-8, Vol. I, f. 70; printed in Maidment, pp. 31–33.

[2] *Caii Julii Caesaris et A. Hirtii de rebus a Caesare gestis Commentarii*, R. and A. Foulis, Glasgow, 1750, folio. The Foulis Press also published quarto and duodecimo editions in the same year.

way, and what Antiquarian Books he has, have meerly got into his Library by Accident.—You may expect more satisfaction from your Friend Mr Gough, than any person I [know.] However when I am settled in Town for the Winter, I shall with great pleasure endeavour to procure you all the Information in my power, on these or any other Subjects, that you will prescribe to me. | I have looked [p. 3.] over the Inscription of the Ring and am of opinion that except the First Second, and Fourth Divisions, which I have attempted to explain, all the rest are meerly ornamental Flourishes. If the Second has any meaning it is probably 𝕮𝖗 i.e. C R, the Initials of *Christus*.— The First is evidently the common old Cypher Iης which some interpret *Iesus Hominum Salvator,* others IHS, the three first Letters of the Greek Iησυς, *Jesus,* this will agree with C R for *Cristus,* as it was often defectively written by the ignorant Monks.—M R is evident enough for *Maria* or perhaps *Maria Regina.* My own opinion is that whole is *JES. CR. Jesus Christus* and *MR* Maria.—And that it is in vain to look for anything further in this relique of antiquity.

Inclosed I send a Letter,[3] which I should be glad to have presented [p. 4.] to the Gentlemen who have the Care of the Advocates Library, thro' their Librarian. Be pleased to show it Mr Davidson and if he thinks it will do desire him to seal it up, and back it with his Interest. Give my best Respects to that Gentleman and all my friends at Edinburgh. I am leaving this place and beg your next letter may be inclosed and in a Cover directed to me as below.

I am Dear Sir
Your most obliged Servant
Th° Percy

To
The Earl of Sussex
at Easton Mauduit
Near Castle Ashby   P.
Northamptonshire.

[3] Printed *infra.*

[*Enclosure* [4]]

Alnwick Castle: Oct. 23 1773

Sir,[5]

The very obliging Manner in which I have been indulged with the Loan of the MS. Collection of ancient Poems, I must ever acknowledge as a very peculiar favour: It has happened however most unfortunately that I have been dissappointed in my expectations of obtaining sufficient Leisure this Summer to make the use of it I intended: My attendance on the Duke of Northumberland has occasioned me to be absent from home much longer this year than usual: and if it would not be too much trespassing upon the Indulgence of the Gentlemen who have the superinten[d]ence of your excellent Library, I should be extremely grateful if they would allow me to retain the Book a little longer than the time assigned: I make this request however with the greatest deference to them, and be it granted or not, shall ever acknowledge myself

Sir

Their and Your

Most obliged humble

Servant

Thomas Percy

[4] *Source:* National Library of Scotland, MS. 1254, No. 53; printed in Maidment, p. 34.

[5] The letter was delivered to Mr. Brown, Librarian to the Faculty of Advocates. See Letter LI *infra*, and Letter XLVII, n. 3, p. 67.

LI
From Paton[1]

[October 26, 1773]

Dear Sir

Your agreeable Favours of 23ᵈ Current came to Hand yesterday, and as Mʳ Davidson is still in the Country did not delay presenting your Letter to Mʳ Brown Librarian to the Faculty of Advocates, who after returning you Compliments for your most polite Letter assured me that in a few Days he was in Expectation to be with some of the principal Curators, to whom your Request would be communicated. he makes no Doubt of it's being granted, how soon this happened he promises to write you.

I have several Weeks ago put into Mʳ Davidson's Hands a Copy of *Forduni Scoti Chronicon,* and shall make Search for Caesar as you describe which will be also consigned there.

Accept of Thanks for the Explanation of the Ring's Inscription, your Sentiments in the greater part agree with mine, be pleased to receive some more of the Impressions,[2] when more is required you shall share of the few by me. | You shall be remember'd to your [p. 2.] Friends and will write you soon again. I am

Dear Sir

Your most obedient Servᵗ

GPaton

Customhouse Edinburgh
   26 October 1773

---

[1] *Source:* British Museum, Add. MS. 32332, f. 53.
[2] Printed slips with the description of the Ring of Alva.

LII

From Paton[1]

Customhouse Edinburgh
15 Nov[r] 1773

Dear Sir

I hope you received my last addrest for You in Northamptonshire, it's now with Pleasure that the inclosed is conveyed wherein M[r] Brown gives you Liberty of retaining the M.S.S. Collection of Songs and Poems for some Months longer. I did not hesitate a Post in conveying you this good Intelligence.

It will be very obliging to clear up this Difficulty whether has L[d] Hailes mistaken the Name instead of George Bannantyne [2] ought it not to be *John Ballenden* as the Author of the *Biographia Britannica* [3] *Vol. 1 p 460, 461,* and so he is inserted in the Additional Volume just now printing of the Advocates Liberary Catalogue. Of this when most convenient and shall be glad to hear from you after you're fixt in London and will write M[r] Gough that you will be soon there that he may have an Opportunity of waiting on you.

M[r] Davidson is come to Town, mentioned the Caesar but he join'd me in dissatisfaction with it, this Copy has no Elegance to induce a Purchaser to pay so high for it the Type being too small for a 4[to]. M[r] Boswell is also returned safely after his dangerous Voyage to Sky with D[r] Johnson.[4] I am with the greatest respect   D[r] Sir

Your most obedient humble
Serv[t] GPaton

---

[1] *Source:* British Museum, Add. MS. 32332, f. 54.

[2] In Hailes's edition of *Ancient Scottish Poems*, 1770, Bannatyne is called Ballantine in the Preface. See Letter XLI, n. 3, p. 59.

[3] *Biographia Britannica: or The*

Lives of the most eminent Persons who have flourished in Great Britain and Ireland, 1747–66, folio, 6 vols.

[4] They crossed to Skye on 2 September 1773 and were in Edinburgh again on 9 November.

Address: To The Revd Dr Thomas Percy

[*Enclosure*^5]

[November 15, 1773]

Revd Doctor

Some weeks ago I received your letter from Mr George Paton: it was laid before the Gentlemen who have the immediate direction of our Library, and, sensible of the reasonableness of your Request, they have desired me to inform you that you have their permission to use Banantyn's MSS. Poems for two or three Months longer

    I am

              Revd Doctor

        Your most obd^t humble Servt

          Alexander Brown

Edin^r 15th

  Novr 1773

Address: To The Revd Doctor Thomas Percy at Alnwick Castle

LIII

From Paton^1

[November 16, 1773]

Dear Sir

Permit me to ask Pardon for omitting the Mark of (P) upon the Letter sent last Night under Cover to the E. of Sussex, which covered Mr Brown the Librarian's Allowance from the Curators

---

^5 *Source:* British Museum, Add. MS. 32332, f. 56.

^1 *Source:* British Museum, Add. MS. 32332, f. 58.

of the Advocate's Liberary to retain the M.S.S. Collection of Poems some Months longer, shall be very happy it reaches you in Course and yields the desired Satisfaction. I write this in Case it has not been delivered to you thro' my Mistake being hurried to overtake the Post of last Night. I ever am

> Revd Dear Sir
> Your most obedient and obliged
> humble Servant   GPaton

Customhouse Edinburgh
  16 Novem^r 1773

PS. If you desire to see Ld *Elibank's Letter to* Ld *Hailes* [2] on his late Publication, (a Copy of which I know was ordered to be delivered to you at London) I shall send one to you under Mr Gough's Cover.

GP

Address: To The Reverend Dr Thomas Percy

LIV

From Paton[1]

[December 27, 1773]

Dear Sir

I hope you received my Letter covering Mr Brown's Answer about the further Indulgence from the Advocate's Liberary to retain the *"M.SS. by Bannantyne."*

It will give me Pleasure to compleat Sir David Lindsay's Satyres,[2]

[2] *A Letter to Sir D. Dalrymple, Lord Hailes, on his Remarks on the History of Scotland*, Edinburgh, 1773, 12°, by Patrick Murray, fifth Baron Elibank.

[1] *Source:* British Museum, Add. MS. 32332, f. 60.
[2] See Letter XLII, n. 2, p. 61.

which are still in Mr Gough's hands and will be delivered to you when you are at leisure to look into them further, for that purpose shall write him so in my next.

You will have sent you by Mr Payne for your Acceptance from me Monro's Account of the Western Isles [3] &^c and Ld Elibank's Letter to Ld Hailes on the late publication. May the Compliments of the Season attend you. I am

Revd Dear Sir
Your most obliged humble
Servt   GPaton

Customhouse Edinburgh
  27 December 1773

Address: To The Reverend Dr Thomas Percy
      Northumberland House
      London

LV

From Percy [1]

Easton Maud^t Feb.6.1774.

Dear Sir,

I blush to look back on the date of your obliging Letter: but hope you will pardon my long Silence, when I inform you that it has been

---

[3] *A Description of the Western Isles of Scotland: Called Hybrides. Compiled by Mr Donald Monro, Dean of the Isles, who travelled through many of them, 1594. Printed in the Year M.DCC.LXXIII*, pp. 1–48. It is the first of four tracts published in one volume, Edinburgh, 1774, 8°. A pen-ciled note on the inside cover of the Bodleian Library copy (G.A. Scotland 8°, 107) states, "Only 50 copies printed."

[1] *Source:* National Library of Scotland, MS. 29-5-8, Vol. I, f. 71; printed in Maidment, pp. 35–36.

owing to my having left London before your letter reached it, which occasioned some delay; and since I have been very much indisposed and all writing forbidden me.[2]

I have received your obliging Letter inclosing the further Indulgence from the Governors of the Advocates' Library, and have the most grateful Sense of their goodness: which I shall be careful [p. 2.] not to abuse, if I have neglected to express it, I beg you | will convey my most respectful sentiments to those Gentlemen, which I shall endeavour to express myself when I return their Book.

My absence of 6 Weeks from London has prevented me from seeing any of the Books you have been so good as to send me; but doubt not their being safe at Northumberland House, where I shall expect to find them on my return to London in the course of next Week.—Be pleased to write to Mr Gough to desire him to send *Lindsay's Satyres* to me at Northumberland House without delay, [p. 3.] that I may compare the imperfect printed | Copy, with the compleat one in Bannatyne's MS.—As the time draws near for my return of that MS. no time should be lost.

—I am truly sensible of all your most obliging favours and remain, with great regard,

Dear Sir

Your very faithful

and most obliged Servant

Tho. Percy

PS/

Will you do me the favour to forward the inclosed Letter by the post, to Mr Hastings?[3] And deliver the other as directed

---

[2] Percy's *Journal* for this period (there is a gap of some eight months) gives no clue to the nature of his illness.

[3] Unidentified.

LVI
From Paton[1]

[February 14, 1774]

Dear Sir

Your most agreeable Favours came to hand last Post and presume on your Goodness to give Currency to the Inclosed, which will bring you soon *Sir David Lindsay's Satyres* from M*r* Gough.

I have communicated your Letter to the Librarian to the Faculty of Advocates, who gives me Leave to inform you that for a Week or two or some more Space beyond your indulged Time, there will be no Scruple to keep *Banantyne's M.SS. Poems*, only be pleased to cause it be carefully packt up in a Box to preserve it from Moisture and Wet when it is returned to me.

Whatever you may chuse from this shall give me a particular pleasure to serve you with: most heartily do I congratulate your Recovery from your Indisposition, wishing you a confirmed State of Health with the Enjoyment of every Blessing.

The Letters were duely forwarded agreeable to the Addresses. I am

Dear Sir
Your most obliged obedient
humble Servt*t*   GPaton

Customhouse Edinburgh
   14 Feb*r* 1774

Address: To The Reverend D*r* Thomas Percy
          Northumberland House
          London

Docket: M*r* Paton
     1774

---

[1] *Source:* British Museum, Add. MS. 32332, f. 62.

LVII
From Paton[1]

[March 1, 1774]

Revd Dear Sir

I hope you would receive my Answer to your agreeable Favours, when you arrived in London.

Presume to inclose a Sale Catalogue if it present any thing worth your Notice be kind enough as let me know and shall endeavour to cause set them aside for you: the Remainder shall come in Course: it will be obliging to permit Mr Gough a Sight of it, I blush to put you to this Trouble have not a Frank Cover so large as to serve him with a Copy. I ever am

Dear Sir

Your most obliged and obedient

humble Servant   GPaton

Edinburgh 1 March
    1774

Address: To The Reverend Dr Thomas Percy
    Northumberland house
    London

[1] *Source:* British Museum, Add. MS. 32332, f. 64.

LVIII

From Percy[1]

Northumberland House,
March 24. 1774.

Dear Sir,

How extremely am I obliged to you on all occasions? I was indeed under some solicitude lest I should exceed my time in detaining the MS. when your kind Letter so agreeably relieved me from all my anxiety on that account. This further indulgence which you have now procured me, is the more agreeable, as for these 2 Months past my attention has been called off from that and all other literary Objects, by a severe illness in my family, which after threatning the life of almost all my Children, at length robbed me of one of them:[2] so that I have scarce | looked into the MS. for some time past.—Yet, [p. 2.] I should not have presumed to have troubled the Librarian with further requests to have it lent me for a longer term; Which makes the favour, so obligingly granted unasked, doubly welcome; and I beg you will let that gentleman know how truly sensible I am of his great politeness and generosity.

I have not a Wish to detain the MS. longer than till next June: but as towards the end of that Month, this family will be removing down to Alnwick Castle, there to spend the Summer; I should be glad if I may be allowed to keep and bring the Manuscript down with me into Northum- | berland, (which I consider almost in your [p. 3.] neighbourhood,) and thence to transmit it by some very certain and safe hand, which cannot fail to offer in the course of the summer: rather than trust it to the conveyance [3] of a common Carrier from

---

[1] *Source:* National Library of Scotland, MS. 29-5-8, Vol. I, ff. 72–73; printed in Maidment, pp. 36–38.

[2] The child was Hetty (b. 4 July 1774), who "died of the Chin Cough, being not quite two years old when she had just begun to prattle and be very engaging." Letter from Henry Percy to William Cleveland, 30 August 1774. See Alice C.C. Gaussen, *Percy: Prelate and Poet*, 1908, p. 125.

[3] After "accidental" deleted.

London.—Nay it is not impossible but [4] before Summer is over, I may be able to bring it with me to Edenborough, in a Post-Chaise myself, which will be still more satisfactory provided the Gentlemen who favoured me with the Loan of it, may not think I detain it from them too long; by waiting for such an opportunity.

Be pleased to mention this to them, and favour me with their final Directions, which I shall most implicitly observe; and remain most [p. 4.] gratefully,

Dear Sir
Their and Your
Most obliged humble
Servant
Thomas Percy

PS/
I was much obliged to you for favouring me with the sight of the Catalogue: tho' I did not find any article, which I particularly wanted.—I should be glad if you could procure me Mr Lambe's battle of Flodden [5] but not without you suffer me to repay you for that and the other articles, you are so good as to procure me.

My best and kindest Respects to my much loved Friends D^r and Mrs Blair.

[p. 5.]   Thursday Evening.
Since I wrote the inclosed Letter, I have received the two Books, which you mentioned in your former Letter to have sent me, viz. (1) The Description of the Western Isles. (2) The Letter to Sr David Dalrymple on his Remarks on Scottish Hist. I must insist upon repaying you these obliging Disbursements.

Address: [6] George Paton Esqr
Custom House
Edingburgh

---

[4] Over "that" deleted.
[5] *An Exact And Circumstantial History of the Battle of Flodden. In Verse. Written About The Time Of* *Queen Elizabeth . . . with Notes By Robert Lambe,* Berwick and London, 1774, 8°. See Letter I, n. 2, p. 1.
[6] The address is not in Percy's hand.

LIX
From Paton[1]

[March–April, 1774 [2]]

Rev[d] Dear Sir

You will please receive the Rest of M[r] Lambe's Battle of Flodden for your Acceptance, which hope will reache you in safety.

I have now the Pleasure to inform you that the Librarian of the Faculty of Advocates indulges your retaining *the M.SS*, till your own Convenience permits you either to bring it North with you to Alnwick Castle, (where you purpose to be this Summer or Autumn) or from thence transmit it to this Place as best suites your Choice of Safety: it gives me Joy to be any how accessory to procure your Wish.

Heartily wishing Health to you and Family, shall always value it a singular Happyness to be of any Service to you, being

Dear Sir

Your most obedient and obliged

humble Servant   GPaton

PS. A new Edition of the old Scot's Songs [3] is soon to be reprinted and then the 2[d] Volume will follow of which afterwards

Address: To The Rev[d] D[r] Thomas Percy
Northumberland House
London

---

[1] *Source:* British Museum, Add. MS. 32332, f. 66.

[2] After Percy's letter of 24 March 1774.

[3] See Letter XI, n. 4, p. 20.

LX
From Percy[1]

Northumberland House, May 14. 1774.

Dear Sir,

You must have thought me guilty of very great Neglect, to have let all your obliging Favours remain so long unacknowledged: but when they arrived I was absent on a Journey into Sussex, and after I came back I could not immediately get a Frank, the Duke having the Gout in his hands. Be pleased to accept my best thanks for the Copy of the Poem on Flodden Field; but it has very much vexed me [p. 2.] that I should give you the trouble to send | me a Copy out of Scotland, when I could have purchased one at our very door here in London: It was owing to meer oversight and inattention that I so inadvertently consented to your taking that trouble upon you, and beg for the future that you will not suffer me to act so unreasonably and foolishly by you. As the Duke is also much absent, I must for the future discontinue using his privilege for the conveyance of any thing but meer Letters; for he was at Newmarket when some of the [p. 3.] Packets | came and at the same time I was absent in Sussex,[2] so that the taking care of the Packets for me created him a good Deal of Embarrassment and Trouble.—A Single Letter, with another single Letter inclosed to any Friend of yours in London, I shall very thankfully receive at any time under his Grace's Cover and will carefully forward as you direct, but any other sort of Packets, or even, Catalogues, I must beg the favour to have sent by the Carrier and I shall with the utmost pleasure pay the Carriage, be it what it will.

[p. 4.]   —How shall I be able to make proper returns for so many obliging favours as you are continually heaping upon me? I wish you

---

[1] *Source:* National Library of Scotland, MS. 29-5-8, Vol. I, f. 74; printed in Maidment, pp. 39–41.

[2] Percy was in Sussex 4–9 April 1774: see Gaussen, *Percy*, p. 169.

would think of any of our London Publications, that I might send you: at least I shall entreat your acceptance of a Set of the New Edition of my Ancient Reliques, which Mr Dodsley is going soon to commit to the Press.³—I thank you a thousand times for the Extension of my time of keeping the old MS. which you have procured for me and desire you will present my best thanks to the Superintendent of the Advocates Library, for his very kind Indulgence: Whatever Pieces I publish from that MS. I shall certainly (as in Duty bound) present to you both and to the Library.

I am
Dear Sir
Your most obliged Servant
T. Percy

LXI

From Percy¹

Alnwick Castle, July 21. 1774

Dear Sir,

I came here a few days ago and brought with me Bannatyne's MS. which has been so long and so obligingly lent me out of your excellent Advocate's Library. I intend to devote a good part of my leisure time during my Summer Residence here to the final Examination of this curious Collection of Ancient Poetry, and then consign it to your care (in consequence of your most obliging permission) to have it returned to the Librarian, whose great politeness and civility I am highly bound to acknowledge, as I am that of all the other Gentlemen who superintend that most valuable repositary.

I flatter myself I shall be able to accompany it with a Copy of the [p. 2.]

³ The third edition of the *Reliques*, land, MS. 29-5-8, Vol. I, f. 75;
1775.   printed in Maidment, pp. 41–43.
¹ *Source:* National Library of Scot-

Houshold Book,[2] for your acceptance, but this *"entre nous;"* for his Grace has so few left, and so many Applications from his friends, that it is difficult to procure one; so that altho' I have long wished to obtain one for you, till now I have not been able to succeed.

Pray how does the Publication of the 2^d Vol. of Scottish Songs,[3] 12 mo. go on: You some time ago promised to procure me a sight of the Manuscript: if it could be forwarded to me here, I have more leisure to overlook it than I usually have in the South. What other literary Works are carrying on in Scotland? What Publications have you had lately? What use do your Booksellers and those at Glasgow [p. 3.] mean to make of the liberty they have gained,[4] by the defeat of our London Booksellers? What new Editions of English Authors [5] are they preparing in consequence of that Victory? Such as are elegant and cheap, one would be glad to purchase.

Adieu! my dear Sir, and favour at your leisure, with a Line

Your very faithful

and obliged Servant

Thos. Percy

PS/

Pray give my best Respects to Mr Boswell: tell him I left Johnson well, preparing to set out with Mrs Thrale for Wales,[6] about a fort-

---

[2] This was not sent. In a letter to Gough, 29 April 1777, Paton refers to "the Northumberland Household Book, which I never saw but once for a short space: hope to be indulged in looking at it again some time this Summer" (National Library of Scotland, MS. 29-5-7, Vol. I, n.f.). A copy is included in the sale catalogue of Paton's library, 1811.

[3] See Letters LXVIII, p. 101 and LXIX, p. 103.

[4] The defeat of the English booksellers' claim to perpetual copyright, by decision of the House of Lords, February, 1774. The struggle with the Scottish booksellers had gone on for thirty years.

[5] *The British Poets,* issued at Edinburgh in 1773 in forty-four thin octavo volumes. This edition was supervised by Hugh Blair. (See *Hugh Blair,* by Robert Morell Schmitz, New York, 1948, pp. 69–71.) Its success led to the *Poets of Great Britain,* printed at Edinburgh (Apollo Press) for John Bell of London, 1776. This was followed by a rival London edition, *Works of the English Poets* (1779–81), for which Johnson wrote prefatory "Lives," later collected in four volumes as *The Lives of the most eminent English Poets,* 1781, 8°.

[6] Johnson set out from Streatham for Wales on 5 July.

night ago. He has begun to print the Account of his Tour thro' the
Highlands.[7] | Is there any Sale of Books going forward at Edin- [p. 4.]
burgh? Your Booksellers could perhaps forward a Catalogue to our
Bookseller Mr Graham [8] at Alnwick? Could you procure me a
Copy of the folio Edition of Fordun at a reasonable Price?

Address: To George Paton Esq
         at the Custom House
         Edinburgh.

LXII
From Paton[1]

[July 26, 1774]

Dear Sir

Some Days have past since I was obliged with your agreeable
Favours of 21st Current, am happy that you are now retired to the
Country where you will find Leisure to look over the Collection of
ancient Poetry undisturbed, your Period of returning it is unconfined
to any Day so you may with all manner of Freedom peruse it till your
intended Time of Returning to London; when you may please consign it to my Care and it shall be punctually lodged again in the
Advocate's Library, and take this opportunity of assuring you that
this is the desire of the Librarian since the Receipt of your last.

Your very kind Remembrance of me commands Thanks of Gratitude which never shall be forgotten, shall be sorry to incommode his
Grace or you any manner of way.

Altho' I've always had in Eye a desire of serving you with
Fordoni Scotichronicon 2 Vol. folio, it | has not hitherto been in my [p. 2.]

[7] *A Journey to the Western Islands
of Scotland,* 1775, 8°. The first sheets
were sent to the press on 20 June
1774; the book was published in January 1775.

[8] Alexander Graham (d. 1789),
bookseller in Alnwick from about
1746.

[1] *Source:* British Museum, Add.
MS. 32332, ff. 68–69.

power to do it, with a Copy that pleased me, but hope before you quit Alnwick Castle to procure you one, of which in due Time.

I believe the Publication of the Scots' Songs is delayed for some time as one of the Company Printers has been in England for some months past, how soon I can obtain the perusal of the Second Volume being the M.SS. of them will insist on it's having a Conveyance to your Place.

At present there is no remarkable Sale Catalogue of Books here, if there be any I shall cause hand one to Mr Graham of your Place.

I hear of no republication of any thing carrying on at present only a set of the English Poets from Milton's Time to the present [2] 20 Vol. of which are already finished in neat enough Pocket Pot 8^{vos}.[2a] Wish the late Victory in the Literary way may be prudently conducted, as a rash incaution may injure more than some do conceive, from the multiplicity of Editions, as too many do often attempt the

[p. 3.] same Book which is | injudicious: any work worthy of Notice I shall inform you of in Course.

I communicated in a Card to Mr Boswell your Paragraph relating to him and Mr Johnson's intended Publication of his Tour [3] thro' the Highlands, this will be eagerly expected by many here, and cannot deny myself to be one of the Number.

Some days ago in looking over Doctor Mead's Catalogue [4] of his Books sold several Years ago by Auction, I found p 233 N° 2492 amongst the 8vo *Songs and Sonnets by Earl of Surry printed 1585*,[5] which sold for £ 1.0.0, if not mistaken this is the Book you some time

---

[2] See Letter LXI, n. 5, p. 90.

[2a] Octavos of the smallest size. The "pot" was a watermark and came to signify a sheet size.

[3] When it was published, Paton observed in a letter to Gough (9 February 1775), "Dr. Johnson's Tour has appeared here, but few is the Number have not seen it, but in general creates much disgust at the time." (National Library of Scotland, MS. 29-5-7, Vol. I, n.f.).

[4] The great Collection of Dr.

Richard Mead (1673–1754) was disposed of in two sales, the first beginning 18 November 1754 and lasting twenty-eight days; the second beginning 7 April 1755 and lasting twenty-nine days. See Nichols's *Literary Anecdotes of the Eighteenth Century*, VI, 218.

[5] See Letter XL. Percy had already been able to borrow copies of this edition. See Percy-Farmer *Correspondence*, p. 101.

ago wrote me about, since the period you mentioned the Book to me, I never could see it any where mentioned; it's probable that this Sale Catalogue may be found out yet, from this the Purchaser may be known and possibly the Book traced out, should your anxiety to see these Songs prevail; if you please I shall write to Mr Gough on his Return to London in Winter to assist your Inquiries in this | matter [p. 4.] as he has assiduously traced out some Articles in this way before now: do you permit me to undertake this Task, I am very hopefull Mr Gough will chearfully contribute his Aid, and you may depend on't it will be a pleasure to me to be of any Service in this or any other way as far as lies in my power.

I shall be always happy to hear from you as Convenience permits being

Revd Sir

Your most obedient and very

much obliged humble Servant

GPaton

Customhouse Edinburgh
   26 July 1774

LXIII

From Paton[1]

[August 6, 1774]

Dear Sir

This day the Waggoner received a Bundle from the King's Printer [2] here for Mr William Cay [3] Bookseller Alnwick in which Parcel I caused put in a Parcel addrest for You, which hope will reach you in

---

[1] *Source:* British Museum, Add. MS. 32332, f. 70.
[2] Alexander Kincaid (1711–77).

[3] William Cay and Company, booksellers, Alnwick (*fl.* 1767–74).

safety it contains Goodall Forduni Scotichronicon 2 Vol. folio for your Acceptance from me.

I have never had an opportunity of meeting the Collector of the Scot's Songs hitherto but expect it soon, from whom hope to get you a Sight of what is so far collected and sent up to Alnwick, if he will consent me this Favour, which I value doing him a singular Service that you have the perusal of it.

Should you have as much leizure as to point out to me the different [p. 2.] Places in *Ballenden's* [4] | *M.SS. Collection of Poems,* belonging to the Advocates' Liberary, from whence I may at my convenience copy out, what shall make *Sir David Lindsay's printed Satires* complete, I shall be most particularly obliged to you, which note may accompany the Book when you will think proper to return, but not till you are fully served with the Loan or Use thereof.

I am with the greatest respect

Dear Rev[d] Sir

Your most obedient and obliged

humble Serv[t]   GPaton

Customhouse Edinburgh
    6 August 1774

PS. If M[r] Gough return'd Lindsay's Satires 4[to] it may be sent me with the M.SS. Collection of Poems as you think proper. *GP*

LXIV

From Percy [1]

Alnwick Castle, Aug[st] 9th 1774

Dear Sir,

I am extremely obliged to you for your constant Attention to every little Persuit of mine: as to the Copy you mention of *Surrey's Poems,*

---

[4] The Bannantyne MS. See Letter XLI, n. 3, p. 59.

[1] *Source:* National Library of Scot-

land, MS. 29-5-8, Vol. I, f. 76; printed in Maidment, pp. 43–44.

it will not be necessary as I have more authentic ones and of a much earlier date.[2] Otherwise I should in consequence of your kind hint apply to M[r] Gough myself without suffering you to give yourself so much trouble.—I have received M[r] Bell's [3] Catalogue, which you have been so good as to send me, and should be glad if you could procure me the Books mentioned on the other side and get them sent to Alnwick, by M[r] Bell directed to the Care of M[r] Graham Bookseller at Alnwick in Northumberland, by whom I will remit the Money. I am

Dear Sir
Your most obliged Servant
Tho[s] Percy

PS/   [p. 2.]
May I beg the favour of a Line to inform me what of these Books I may expect and when, and if you have not already bought me the folio Edition of Fordun, you need not now buy it: if you do buy Fordun or cannot dispose of it again, then I would omit having *Abercrombie* in the opposite List.

NB If N° 1480 contains the 2 parts I should be particularly glad to secure that.

M[r] Bell's Catalogue   [p. 3.]
N° 19.Sibbaldi Scotia illustrata.[4] ———— 7 : 6
107.Crawfurd's Peerage [5] ———— 10 : 0
422.Sir Percy Herbert [6] &c ———— 1 : 0

---

[2] For a list of the early editions located by Percy, see Percy-Farmer *Correspondence*, p. 196.

[3] John Bell (*c*. 1736–1806), bookseller and publisher in Edinburgh. See G. H. Bushnell, *Dictionary of Printers from 1726 to 1775* (Bibliographical Society), Oxford, 1930, pp. 282–83. He is not to be confused with the more famous John Bell of Exeter Change, Strand, London.

[4] Sir Robert Sibbald (1641–1722), *Scotia Illustrata, Sive Prodromus Historiæ Naturalis*, Edinburgh, 1683, folio. The author's copy, with many alterations and additions evidently in preparation for a new edition, is preserved in the library of the University of St. Andrews, Typ. BE. C84. K8.

[5] George Crawfurd (d. 1748), genealogist, *The Peerage of Scotland*, Edinburgh, 1716, folio.

[6] *Certaine Conceptions or Considerations of Sir Percy Herbert upon the strange change of Peoples dispositions and actions in these latter times*, 1652, 4°.

678 Cornwath's Memoirs [7] &c ————— 2 : 6
1274.History of the Rebellion [8] &c ——— 2 : 0
1480.Vida de Lazarillo [9] &c ————————— 1 : 0
   (Please to see that this contains
   the second Part, else do not buy
   it.)
1578 Lettres historiques &c des Revol.[10]   1 : 0
   37.Drummond of Hawthornden [11] — 7 .
   111.Abercrombie. 2 Vol.[12] ————————— 14 —
   282.Nesbit's Essay [13] ——————————————— 3 .
   286 Life of Wallace [14] ———————————————— 5
   287 Life of Bruce [15] ——————————————— 5 .

LXV

From Paton[1]

[August 11, 1774]

Dear Sir

Agreeable to your Favours of 9th Current I have caused lay side, to be sent you per [2] first Waggon from this, the following Books

[7] George Lockhart of Carnwath (1673–1731), *Memoirs Concerning the Affairs of Scotland,* 1714, 8°; third edition, 1714.

[8] Andrew Henderson (*fl.* 1734–75), bookseller and miscellaneous writer. *The history of the rebellion, 1745 and 1746 . . . ,* Edinburgh, 1748, 12°.

[9] *La Vida de Lazarillo de Tormes, y de sus fortunas y adversidades,* Anvers, 1554–55, 12°, 2 parts.

[10] Cannot be identified with certainty.

[11] *The Works of William Drummond of Hawthornden,* Edinburgh, 1711, folio.

[12] Patrick Abercromby (1656–1716?), graduate of the University of St. Andrews, antiquary, historian, physician. He practiced medicine in Edinburgh. *The martial atchievements of the Scots nation,* Edinburgh, 1711–15, folio, 2 vols.

[13] Alexander Nisbet (1657–1725), heraldic writer, *Essay on the ancient and modern use of Armories,* Edinburgh and London, 1718, 4°.

[14] See Letter LXV, n. 3, p. 97.

[15] *Ibid.*

[1] *Source:* British Museum, Add. MS. 32332, f. 71.

[2] Paton here makes use of a special character something like a Greek *phi.*

of your List, which remained unsold yesterday and are these vizt.

107	Crawford's Peerage fol. bd	£—.	10. —
282	Nisbett's Essay on Armories 4to St	—.	3. —
286	Life of Wallace 4to boards	—.	5. —
287	—— of Bruce 4to d°	—.	5. —
422	Sir Percy Herbert & 4to	—.	1. —
628	Carnwath's Memoirs 8° bd	—.	2. 6
1274	History of the Rebellion 12°	—.	2. —
		£ 1.	8. 6

Sibbaldi Scotia Illustrata fol. Lettres Historiques &^{ca} and Drummond of Hawthorden were sold some time ago, and Vida de Lazarillo &c^a has been mislaid, so as not to be got, however I suspect it to be no more than a part of the Book, have given orders should it cast up, to inform me, of which I shall afterwards write you.

I past over Abercrombie's Martial Atchievements 2 Vol. fol. as one of the Volumes is only Sticht, the other bound, besides hope by this time or before this reache you, Forduni Scotichronicon may have come to hand.

Mr Boswell offers his Compliments, is desirous to know if you [p. 2.] intend to visit this Country any time this Autumn, promised (if this Season should be too short for the intended Use you would make of *Ballenden's M.SS. Collection of Poems*) to obtain a prolongation of Time, that you might thoroly examine it or copy out what you require.

I have to observe that there is no Titlepage to Bruce's Life, none being ever printed for it, both these Lives being never properly finished by the first Undertaker Mr *Robert Freebairn* [3] late King's Printer in Scotland, whose Affairs did not permit him to finish his Plan and as these now appear were sold to some of the Trade here and are become pretty scarce: the other Life has a Titlepage to promote the Sale.

---

[3] Robert Freebairn (*fl.* 1740). This is the accepted account of these publications. See *The Bruce and Wallace*, ed. John Jamieson, Edinburgh, 1820, 4°, 2 vols., "Preliminary Remarks," II, ix.

Forgive the Freedom used of inclosing this for Mr Graham [4] to whose Care the Parcel will be recommended. I am

Dear Sir
Your most obedient Servant
GPaton

Customhouse Edinburgh
11 August 1774

Address: To The Reverend Dr Thomas Percy
Alnwick Castle
Northumberland

LXVI

From Percy[1]

Alnwick Castle, Aug. 18. 1774.

Dear Sir,

How much am I obliged to you for the innumerable favours you incessantly heap upon me?—I have received *Fordun's Scoti-chronicon,* and hope soon to receive the other Parcels, both Printed Books and the MS. Songs.—

I am equally obliged to you with regard to *Fordun,* as if I accepted it in the kind manner you intended; but as I never wanted it for myself, only to supply another Person, I must beg to know what it cost you, that I may pay for it with the other Books. This I must beg leave to insist upon.—I am, however, but too much obliged to you already for your many former favours.

[p. 2.]   I unluckily left your printed Copy of Lindsey's Satirical Play in

---

[4] See Letter LXI, *ad fin.*

[1] *Source:* National Library of Scot-

land, MS. 29-5-8, Vol. I, f. 77; printed in Maidment, pp. 45–46.

London: So cannot return it with the MS.² which I will, if possible, endeavour to send before the end of Summer: but I have got a compleat Transcript ³ made by Allan Ramsey, and lent me by his Son.⁴—

I know not whether I have thanked you for your kind offer about Surrey's Poems: but the Copy you mentioned is but an incorrect one and I have some much earlier.—Pray give my best thanks to Mʳ Boswell, for his kind Message about the MS.—*should* it be necessary, I shall apply to him. I write in great haste; but am ever most truly

Dear Sir
Your obliged Servant
Tho. Percy

LXVII

From Paton¹

[August 22, 1774]

Dear Sir

You was kind enough formerly to inform me that you had preferable Editions of Surrey's Poems, than the Copy, which once belonged to Dʳ Mead, and all of them must be very rare.

Please give yourself no uneasyness about *Lindsay's Satirical Play,* any time when most suitable to your Convenience it may be returned, am in no hurry about it, be you fully satisfied with the perusal and afterwards may use the Freedom of informing how it can be sent me.

It is very proper that Mʳ Ramsay has communicated to you his Father's Transcript, from which you will easily observe his Inter-

---

² See Letter XLII, n. 2, p. 61.
³ In the possession of John Cowie, Esq., of Glasgow. A microfilm copy is deposited in the National Library of Scotland. See also *The Bannatyne Manuscript*, ed. Ritchie, 1934, I, xxiii–xxvii.

⁴ Allan Ramsay, the younger (1713–84), artist and portrait painter to George III.
¹ *Source:* British Museum, Add. MS. 32332, f. 73.

polations &cᵃ. I desist saying any more about the M.S.S.—If Mʳ
Boswell still remains in Town shall deliver your Compliments.
I sent you *Forduni Scotichronicon,* and beg your Acceptance of,
shall be happy the Copy satisfies Dʳ Percy or his Friend, being at all
[p. 2.] Times | ready to express my Gratitude for your Favours.
Have you seen *Rolland* ² of Dalkeith *his Poems* of which I am pretty
certain there are two Editions but now very scarce, it is intitled *the
Seven Sages,* first printed by Rob. Smyth at his Buith near the Nether-
bow Edinbʳ 1592 and again by *Andro Hart 1631,* which last I have.
Lately I met with *An essay on Buchanan his Paraphrase on the 1ˢᵗ
twentie Psalmes of David,*³ *translated Lond. 1627 in 12⁰* but there is
41 of them by S.P.L. Pray can you explain this Author's Name to
me? It consists but of 94 pages—In the Volume are several other
Poetical Tracts vizᵗ Musarum Deliciae ⁴ or the Muses Recreation.
containing severale pieces of Poetique Witt 2ᵈ Edition by Jⁿ I. M and
Ia. S. Lond 1656—Men-miracles ⁵ and other poems, &ᶜ.

² *The seuin Seages Translatit out
of prois in Scottis meter be Iohne Rolland in Dalkeith, . . . Imprentit at
Edinburgh be Iohne Ros, for Henrie Charteris. M.D.LXXVIII.* Robert
Smyth's is the second of the known
editions, title page 1592, colophon
1595. Stray leaves of another edition, apparently of the same period
as Smyth's, have been discovered.
Andro Hart published an edition in
1620. The 1631 edition is a reprint
of that. See the edition by George I.
Black (Scottish Text Society), Edinburgh, 1932, xvi–xxv.

³ George Buchanan (1506–82), hu-
manist and reformer, Principal of St.
Leonard's College, St. Andrews, and
tutor to James VI and I. *One and
forty Divine Odes Englished, set
to King Davids Princely Harpe.
By S.P.L. London, Printed by M.F.,
1627, 8⁰,* 3 p. I., 94 p. Signatures:
A-F⁸, G³ (C8 is a blank, not included in paging). On [A2] is an-

other title-page: *An Assay, Or Bvcha-
nan His Paraphrase On the First
twentie Psalmes of David. Translated. London Printed by R.Y. for
Richard Moore . . . ,* 1627. This
title page applies to Part 1, ending on
page 39, [C7ʳ]. Part 2 is on Psalms
21–41; Psalm 21 begins on page 41.
⁴ *Musarum Deliciæ: or, The Muses
Recreation. Conteining severall select
Pieces of Poetique Wit By Sʳ J.M.
and Ja: S.* [Sir John Mennis, 1599–
1671, and Dr. James Smith, 1605–
67], 1656 (second edition) ; edited by
E. Dubois, 1817, 2 vols. There was a
reprint in 1874.
⁵ Martin Lluelyn (1616–82), poet,
physician, and Principal of St.
Mary Hall, Oxford, *Men—Miracles.
With other Poemes. By* M[artin]
Ll[uelyn], St[udent] of Ch[rist]
Ch[urch] in Oxon., 1646, 16⁰. Another edition of *Men—miracles. With
other poemes* [Oxford, by H. Hall]
was printed in 1646, 8⁰.

I beg you Excuse for this Freedom used by

Dear Sir

Your most obedient humble

Servant   GPaton

Customhouse Edinburgh
   22 August 1774

LXVIII

From Percy[1]

Alnwick Castle, Aug. 22^d 1774.

Dear Sir,

My Parcel containing the Books you were so good as to secure for me out of Mr Bell's Sale, and also the MS. Collection of Songs, came safe. I am truly grateful for the trouble you are so good as to give yourself on this and all other occasions to oblige me. I have looked over the MS. Collection of Scottish Songs,[2] and find most of them are Fragments too mutilated and imperfect to afford much pleasure to a reader in their present State, and yet most of them contain charming hints, which might give occasion to very beautiful Songs, if supplied and filled up, in the manner that old broken fragments of antique Statues have been repaired and compleated by modern Masters. I [p. 2.] think I could fill up the breaches of some of them myself,[3] and by waiting a little one might possibly recover more perfect Copies of some of the others: In the meantime it would be pity to delay the publication of the 2^d Vol. of Scottish Songs till these discoveries are made: I

---

[1] *Source:* National Library of Scotland, MS. 29-5-8, Vol. I, f. 78; printed in Maidment, pp. 46–48.
[2] The MS. is now in the British Museum, Add. MSS. 22311–12. See also Hecht, *Songs from David Herd's Manuscripts.*
[3] Percy had made use of this method in his *Reliques.* See Percy-Hailes *Correspondence,* pp. xiii–xiv.

wish you would persuade the Editor to collect all that are tolerably perfect, in this or any other Collection, I would furnish him myself [4] with a good number of old Scots Songs and Poems, all perfect and compleat which have never yet been printed, and which I myself

[p. 3.] transcribed, from an old Manuscript at Cambridge | which was compiled by old Sr Richard Maitland ancestor of the Earls of Lauderdale, and many others might be transcribed by himself from Banatyne's MS. when I return it: all these would easily fill a 2^d Volume forthwith.—As in 3 or 4 years I intend to publish a Volume or Two More of old English and Scottish Poems in the Manner of my *Reliques of Ancient English Poetry,* I shall then insert some of these Fragments if the Editor will give me leave to transcribe and fill up the deficiencies of some of them in the manner I attempted before: and from my

[p. 4.] book he may reprint such | of them as suit his subject and plan, in his 3^d Volume, in like manner as he did in his first Volume. Let me know what he thinks of this proposal and write as soon as possible; because till I hear from you, I shall not presume to touch one of them. I am most truly

Dear Sir

Your very obliged

Servant

T. Percy

PS/

As I make these things only the amusements of my most idle and leisure moments, it will require time to compleat such fragments.

---

[4] Percy was unable to fulfill these promises. See Letter LXXXIII, p. 122, and Appendices I and II, pp. 170, 171, 172.

LXIX
From Paton[1]

[August 29, 1774]

Dear Sir

I would have answered your kind Favours of 22ᵈ Current had I been favoured with a proper Answer earlier, it having only come to my Hand this day, so use the Freedom of inclosing same, Mʳ Herd the Collector of these Songs has given it to the Printer Mʳ Wotherspoon[2] and both give you the Indulgence requested: when convenient or if agreeable your Sentiments shall be communicated in the same way.

You will please to receive also the Paragraph[3] referr'd to in the P.S. which as desired may be returned.

It would be obliging to learn if *Scotland's Complaint*[4] has a place in Sir Richᵈ Maitland's M.S.S. this altho' *printed* is not to be met with any where, and am informed that many Songs or Poems are taken notice of there (for I never saw the small Book) in the same way as Io. Major mentions James I Poem *Peeblis at the Play*,[5] *&ᶜ.* This Tract was promised me by a worthy old Gentleman, whose Search for it proved fruitless and since his decease the Book did not | appear [p. 2.] amongst his Collection, as probably it might have been lost or abstracted thro' the variety of movings from place to place; but if not mistaken he observed many years ago to me that such *Lines of Songs, Poems* &cᵃ were mentioned in this small Composition as our Historian did, leaving Posterity to a vain Search for the Remainder.

I hope my Silence these two three Posts has not occasioned any

---

[1] *Source:* British Museum, Add. MS. 32332, f. 75.

[2] John Wotherspoon (d 1776) of Martin and Wotherspoon, the Apollo Press.

[3] See Appendix I, p. 169.

[4] *The Complaynt of Scotlande,* 1549?, probably printed at Paris. Of the four original copies known to exist, all lack the title page. *The Complaynt* was edited for the E.E.T.S. by James Murray, 1872–73.

[5] See Letter XL, nn. 8 and 9, p. 58.

inconvenience to you, being unable to make the proper reply till now.
I am

> Dear Sir
> Your most obedient humble
> Servant   Gpaton

Customhouse Edinburgh
29 August 1774

Address: To The Reverend Dr Thomas Percy
Alnwick Castle

LXX

From Paton[1]

[September, 12, 1774]

Revd Dear Sir

I am desired to inform you that there will be put into my Hands
a parcel of *Old Historical Scots Ballats,*[2] both printed and Manuscript, which are to be transmitted to you, so beg to know if these
may be sent in parcels by post, or should they come by the Waggon or
Carrier, but am affraid may be lost or mislaid provided the later get
Charge of them, small packets being liable to that misfortune. I wait
your Directions which shall be followed.

It is generally allowed that ——— *Inglis* was Author of *The
Complaint of Scotland,*[3] instead of my writing you formerly that it
was *Maitland.*

---

[1] *Source:* British Museum, Add.
MS. 32332, f. 79.
[2] There is no precise account of
these ballads in the letters which follow. They may have been among the
MSS. and black-letter pamphlets and

ballads lost in the fire at Northumberland House in 1780.
[3] See a concise account of the prob-
lem of the authorship of the *Complaynt* in Henderson's *Scottish Vernacular Literature,* pp. 305–07.

I saw some of the Coins lately found in Orkney [4] these appear to be *Cnut* or *Canute's* Coinage, if I procure any of them, should it be agreeable you shall have one or more of them. I am most respectfully
Dear Sir
Your most obedient humble
Servant   GPaton

Customhouse Edinburgh
  12 September 1774

Address: To The Reverend D[r] Thomas Percy Alnwick Castle Northumberland

LXXI

From Percy[1]

Alnwick Castle Sep. 16. 1774

My dear good Sir,

   I should not have delayed to acknowledge the favour of your former Letters till the arrival of your Last of 12th Inst. had I not been absent on a Tour thr' Cumberland.—I cannot express how much I feel myself obliged to you for your continual attention to gratify me in all Respects. I shall be extremely glad to see the Parcel of old Historicall Ballads, which you mention, in print and Manuscript: but could wish if possible they might rather be sent by the Carrier, than under Cover to his Grace, and if you think the parcel too Small, I would wait | till some more favourable opportunity [p. 2.] offer: but unless it be a single piece or so, now and then inclosed in your Letter, I could rather wish to decline having them sent under his Grace's Covers, as he is often absent and it is troublesome to send packets after him, which are to come back again.—

---

[4] See Letter CII, p. 152.
[1] *Source:* National Library of Scot- land, MS. 29-5-8, Vol. I, f. 79; printed in Maidment, pp. 48–50.

I beg you will present my Compliments to M[r] Wotherspoon together with the inclosed Leaf[2] which contains an hypothesis that [p. 3.] is certainly very ingenious | and probable at least; whether the Oratorio be immediately sprung from the old Mystery or not. He does me great honour in referring to my publication and I shall be very glad to purchase his book when published. I will transmit the Songs when I return to the South.

And now, my Dear Sir, I hope you will pardon my persevering in my Desire to repay you for Fordun, as it is for another person, whom I shall not scruple to make pay for it, and unless you do this, I cannot send it to him, but must return it to Edinburgh. Your great [p. 4.] Generosity | in other Instances, sufficiently distresses me, and you will really render it impossible for me ever to trouble you with my petty commissions any more.—May I beg the favour to trouble you with the enclosed Letter to D[r] Blair to whom I could wish it may be delivered at latest when he comes to preach at his Church next Sunday. I am

> Dear Sir
> Your much obliged
> and ever faithful Servant
> Tho[s] Percy

LXXII

From Paton[1]

[September 24, 1774]

Dear Sir

I ought to have answered your very kind Favours of 16th Current before this time, having waited an opportunity of transmitting the small parcels of Ballads in one to any of the Booksellers in Alnwick,

[2] See Appendix I, p. 169.   [1] *Source:* British Museum, Add. MS. 32332, f. 81.

Morpeth or Newcastle, but none has hitherto offered; should it be the same next week shall forward them by the Carrier then, and inclosed send the List² of such as are put into my hand.

Mʳ Witherspoon³ expresses his Thanks for the notice taken of his Sentiments, seems to be uncertain when the Collection will be finished but shall take care of providing you with a Copy when printed.— You may carry the M.SS. Volume of the Songs South to peruse at your Leisure.

The Letter was conveyed to Dʳ Blair as dircted in yours.

Please know that Fordoun cost nothing so no more can be charged for it; be assured none is so welcome: beg that you will not restrain me the pleasure at any future time of serving you, so look for the continuance of your Commissions, being at all times

Dear Sir

Your most obedient and obliged

humble Servᵗ   GPaton

Customhouse Edinburgh
    24 Septemʳ 1774

Address: To The Reverend Dʳ Thomas Percy
    Alnwick Castle

LXXIII

From Percy¹

Alnwick Castle, Sepʳ 30ᵗʰ 1774

Dear Sir,

I see you will overwhelm me with obligations, which I cannot sufficiently acknowledge, tho' I must most gratefully feel them. I

² This list of ballads is missing.
³ Paton's spelling of Wotherspoon, repeated in Letter LXXIV, indicates his pronunciation.

¹ *Source:* National Library of Scotland, MS. 29-5-8, Vol. I, f. 80; printed in Maidment, pp. 50–52.

really must be more guarded for the future, how I express my Wishes and Desires on any Subject, as you [are] so uncommonly generous and assiduous in gratifying them. Accept a thousand thanks for your most valuable Present since it must be so: and direct me how I can remit you the Money for the rest: perhaps this will be best done by paying it in London to some Bookseller, who corresponds with your's at Edinburgh. We are now preparing to leave this Country for the present year: and therefore, if not already sent by the Carrier, I will [p. 2.] beg | you to send the old Ballads you have been so good as to collect for me, in Letters directed to me, which Letters may be inclosed under Covers, with this Direction

```
To The Earl of Sussex      P
  at Easton Mauduit
  Near Castle Ashby
  Northamptonshire
```

Be careful to add the P—By this Mode of conveyance, you may send as Many Packets, as you please, only let none of them separately exceed 2 ounces. I shall be chiefly at Easton Mauduit till after Christmas, and shall be infinitely obliged to you for any Old Songs, Ballads or Poems which you may chance to pick up either in Print or Manuscript.

[p. 3.]   If I can get time to finish my cursory Perusal of the remaining Songs in Bannatyne's MS. which was so generously lent me out of your Advocate's Library, I will yet send it to you, before I leave this Place; (of which you may expect advice, whenever sent;) If not, as I am pressed for time, I will accept the kind Indulgence of your most obliging Librarian, and detain it a little Longer and so send it from London: which last plan, if you do not hear from me soon, you may conclude, I have adopted. Pray present my best respects and thanks to him for all his Civilities and believe me to be

My dear Sir

Your most obliged and grateful Servant

T. Percy

PS/ [p. 4.]
I shall use Mr Wotherspoon['s] obliging Permission to keep the
MS. Songs by me till wanted.

PS/
We shall certainly depart in less than a fortnight from Alnwick
and therefore after this next Week don't direct to me under Cover
to his Grace any more, till you hear further. Let all your future
Directions be under Cover to the Earl of Sussex.
—Do me the favour to accept the inclosed. I know not whether I
sent it you before or not.

LXXIV

From Paton[1]

[October 3, 1774]

Revd Dear Sir

Your Favours of 30th past covering the acceptable Leafe to your
elegant *Poem of the Hermit of Warkworth*,[2] came to hand for which
be pleased to accept of my best Thanks, this shall be annexed to the
next Edition of that beautifull Piece as I can meet with none in
Town at present, a Lady having carried off the Copy you was so
kind as send me formerly.
The small Parcel went off on Friday last from hence in the

---

[1] *Source:* British Museum, Add.
MS. 32332, ff. 83–84.
[2] *The Hermit of Warkworth. A
Northumberland Ballad. In Three
Fits or Cantos*, 1771, 4°, fourth edi-
tion, 1775. The "leaf" was probably
*A Description of the Hermitage of
Warkworth.* AN EXTRACT OF A LET-
TER FROM *Newcastle-upon-Tyne*,
DATED THE 6TH OF *September, 1771.*
A copy is preserved in the Bodleian
Library (Gough Northumberland 8).
It is bound up with a copy of the first
edition of *The Hermit of Warkworth*
inscribed in Percy's hand "To M^r
Moffat." See Letter XXXII, n. 2,
p. 41.

Waggon for Newcastle *addrest for you at Alnwick Castle*, so hope it may reache your Place by tomorrow or so, as these managers of this Carriage do drop properly Parcels by the way it being marked down in the Book of Articles received for Delivery here.

Your very exact Directions under the Earl of Essex's Cover shall be punctually observed with the Addition of P below the Seal, you may be assured every old Ballad &c that I can meet with shall be [p. 2.] forwarded as advised, and none shall exceed 2 Ounces, this Course I'l observe during your Stay at Easton Mauduit till Christmas.

The Librarian is out at present on an Excursion, I once hoped to have made one of the Party, but Revenue Matters with Attendance at the Exchequer just now disconcerted my Scheme. I wearie much for a very few days' Amusement, but must postpone it till some time hence——. nothing would please so much as viewing your elegant Alnwick Castle, which pleasure would have been the more increased to have kist your hand there: on Mr Brown's Return your Request shall be imparted and persuade myself not without Success: I assuredly know Mr Witherspoon[3] grudges not your keeping the M.SS. Songs, as these must be greatly improved by your correcting hand.

Permit me to solicite the Favour of your Inquiry of His Lordship Percy[4] whether Doctor Alexander Monro Drummond[5] Professor [p. 3.] of Physick and Medicine | in this University was in Company with his Lordship at Cairo, or at any other Place in Egypt, or if Lord Percy hear'd any thing of that Gentleman, his Silence to his Friends and Relations for so long a Time make them extremely anxious: I beg pardon for this piece of trouble, but am importuned by them

[3] Cf. Letter LXXII, n. 3, p. 107.

[4] Lord Algernon Percy (1750–1830), second son of the Earl, later Duke, of Northumberland. In 1790, he was created Earl of Beverley.

[5] Alexander Monro Drummond (1742–82). He was elected Professor of the Institutes of Medicine in the University of Edinburgh in 1773 while resident at the court of the King of Naples. The University au-thorities had difficulty in establishing communication with him and appealed to relatives and intermediaries to help. He did not return to take up his appointment, and on June 19, 1776, Dr. James Gregory was elected in his place. See Andrew Dalzel, *History of the University of Edinburgh*, Edinburgh, 1862, 2 vols., II, Appendix, 442–48.

to make the Inquiry as they are sure [6] that Lord Percy is returned to Britain.

I shall advise you when the Bookseller Mr Bell informs me to whom in London you may pay his Bill, hoping you will not deny me any future opportunity in obeying your welcome Calls for any thing required from hence that I can procure you, being

Dear Sir

Your most obedient and obliged

humble Servt   GPaton

Customhouse Edinburgh
    3 October 1774

Address: To The Reverend Dr Thomas Percy
    Alnwick Castle

LXXV

From Percy [1]

Easton Maudit, Novr 30.1774.

My dear Sir,

I have long wished to do myself the pleasure of writing to you, but being here confined in the Country where I could get no Frank, I could not allow myself to put you to the expence of Postage; but at length I had an opportunity of forwarding this to Alnwick, and then I could delay writing no longer. I have received safe your obliging Present of the old Ballads, which have followed me into the South, and are a new Proof, added to innumerable others, of your kind attention to me and constant wishes to gratify your absent Friends.

---

[6] MS. reads "assure."
[1] *Source:* National Library of Scot-

land, MS. 29-5-8, Vol. I, f. 81;
printed in Maidment, pp. 52–54.

[p. 2.]   Be pleased to observe that any Letter directed to me here, must not be under Cover To the Earl of Essex. but To the Earl of Sussex, and distinguished with a *P,* as I have before remarked.

A long indisposition has prevented me from availing myself so much as I intended, of my Retreat in the Country for literary per-suits: but I hope ere long to be able to resume that kind of Amuse-ments. The same cause has hindered me from making the active Inquiries you desired after Dr Alexander Monro Drummond but [p. 3.] when I get fixed in London for | the remainder of the Winter (which yet will hardly be soon) I will make all the inquiries in my power: as for Lord Algernon he is too remote to apply to him, for we have not yet heard of his getting to France.—Be pleased to men-tion this, together with my kindest and best Respects to my good friend Dr Blair, who in his Letter to me, desired me to make the same Inquiry: tell him I have been drawn in to delay writing to him, in hopes I should have been able to answer his Wishes on this subject long before now.—A lame Leg which I have had these 5 Weeks, I fear will keep me long from London, in the meantime Dr Drummond's Friends surely might apply to Lord Winchelsea's [2] Mother Lady Charlotte Finch at St. James's Palace London, and have their Doubts resolved at once.

I am,

Dear Sir, most truly

Your most obliged Servant

Thomas Percy

Address: To George Paton Esq
at the Custom House,
Edinburgh.

[2] George Finch (1752–1826), Earl of Winchelsea and Nottingham.

LXXVI
From Paton[1]

[December 1, 1774]

Revd Dear Sir

I wrote you on Receipt of your last Favours from Alnwick of 30th September last, which hope reached you, having nothing remarkable offering since that time did not chuse to break in upon your more important Studies, if any Ballads shall afterwards occurr, care will be taken to forward them as you have directed me.

You will please herewith receive a small Auction Catalogue, what may be wanted, be kind enough as inform me and I will endeavour to attend your Orders. Mr Bell informs me if the Amount of his Account is paid into "*Mr Edward Johnston*[2] *Bookseller St Paul's Churchyard London*," it will be acceptable to him, for which take a Receipt for the Sum.

Mr Brown Librarian to the Advocates here presents Compliments desires you need be in no hurry about the Return of *Banatine's Poems M.SS.* if these be wanted he is to inform me in due time.

It will be exceedingly obliging to learn if you have had any Accounts of Dr Alex^r Monro Drummond or if he was in Aegypt, his Relations are in the | utmost pain about him, his Silence having been [p. 2.] so long.

Several Weeks ago the promising Scots poetic Genius Ferguson[3] was cut off by a Fever, so the expected Scheme of Virgil's Ecclogues &c^a to complete Gavin Douglas is at an End.

Who is Editor of the *Prolusions?*[4]

Mr Gough writes me that he has retired to Enfield and scarcely

---

[1] *Source:* British Museum, Add. MS. 32332, f. 87.

[2] Edward Johnson (1709–96), bookseller in London and at one time partner with Benjamin Dodd.

[3] Robert Fergusson (1750–74). See Letter XXXVII, n. 2, p. 53.

[4] *Prolusions; or, select Pieces of antient Poetry*, 1760, 8°, ed. Edward Capell (1713–81).

purposes to reside in London for this Winter, still adheres to his Inquiries.

I am with the greatest respect and gratitude

Dear Sir

Your most obedient and obliged

humble Servt   GPaton

Customhouse Edinburgh

1st Decem^r 1774

LXXVII

From Paton[1]

[December 9, 1774]

Revd Dear Sir

Yesterday I received your most agreeable Favours of 30th past, please let the Want of Franks deny me no Opportunity of hearing from you when convenient or serving you here.

I am glad the Ballads came to hand, nothing new of the kind has cast up since else would have been sent.

Your Correction of my Blunder in the *Address* shall be attended to for the future.

The distress you have been under gives me real pain, but hope the Complaints will be soon removed and give you full Liberty to pursue your literary Inquiries; receive Dr Blair's answer to my Card, having conveyed the Paragraph to him as directed immediately on the Receipt of your Favours and with the good Doctor heartily condole with you in your Distress.

I wish soon the happy Approach of good accounts from Lord Algernon; accept of genuine Thanks for the kind concern about Dr Drummond, whose Silence make all here dread the worst: your

[1] *Source:* British Museum, Add. MS. 323332, f. 85.

Chain of procuring Intelligence is just and will be used. I pray for your perfect recovery and ever am,

Dear Sir Your most obedient hum^le Servant

GPaton

Customhouse Edinburgh
9th October ² 1774

Address: The Reverend Dr Thomas Percy
Easton Mauduit

[*Enclosure* ³]

Dr Blair presents best Comp^ts to Mr Paton—returns him thanks for transmitting to him so carefully what Dr Percy had communicated—He has nothing particular to write on this Occasion to Dr Percy which would deserve a Separate Letter; only begs the favour that Mr Paton when he writes would present Dr Blair's best respects and assure him of his Sincere Concern for the illness which Dr Percy mentions himself to Suffer; together with his thanks for his extended enquiries about Dr Drummond. He is surprised and somewhat Uneasy to be informed that L. Alg. Percy is not yet come to France, as he expected he would have been in England | by this time: [p. 2.] and will be happy to hear from Dr Percy as soon as is Convenient for him good accounts of his health, together with such intelligence as he can give him Concerning Lord Algernon.

Friday

Address: To Mr George Paton
Customhouse

---

² A mistake for December.   ³ *Source:* British Museum, Add. MS. 32332, f. 129.

LXXVIII
From Paton[1]

[December 22, 1774]

Revd Dear Sir

I hope you will receive in safety Mr Balfour's last part of his Sale Catalogue, if any thing is wanted from thence, please write me and it shall be secured and sent to London or as you will be pleased to advise me.

It is with real concern that I inform you that Dr Drummond's Father died yesterday of real Grief for the supposed Loss of his Son about whom Your kind Inquiries were so warmly exprest.

I shall be extremely happy to hear that you regain your former state of good Health, it being the sincere wish, that you ever may be happy, of

Dear Sir
Your most obliged and obedient
humble Servt   GPaton

Customhouse Edinburgh
22 Decem^r 1774

Address: The Reverend Dr Thomas Percy
Easton Mauduit

[1] *Source:* British Museum, Add. MS. 32332, f. 89.

LXXIX
From Percy[1]

Easton Maud^t Decr 31.1774.

My dear good Sir,

How kindly obliging are you to me upon all occasions? I have been favoured with two Catalogues of Books but shall not have occasion to trouble you for any Articles in either of them. I am no less obliged to you for forwarding to me the Card of my good friend Dr Blair, to whom I shall write at large as soon as I can give him any authentic Intelligence of Lord Algernon Percy: but the Duke and Duchess being at Bath, I am not in the way of hearing about his Lordship till we meet in London: then I shall express my kind Sentiments to a man, whom I so truly love and honour. I write in great haste and therefore hope you will pardon the brevity of
Dear Sir
Your most obliged Servant
Thos Percy

PS/   [p. 2.]

Many happy years to you: the same I wish to my friend Dr Blair and his good Spouse, which I hope you will be so kind as to signify to him. I am still a Cripple, but I flatter myself getting better.

Address: To George Paton Esq
at the Custom House
Edinburgh.

---

[1] *Source:* National Library of Scotland, MS. 29-5-8, Vol. I, f. 82;   printed in Maidment, pp. 54–55.

LXXX
From Paton[1]

[January 13, 1775]

Revd Dear Sir

Some days ago I was favoured with yours of 31st ultimo, rejoice to find you are getting the better of your Complaints, wish a speedy and perfect Recovery, that you may be enabled to pass further South and enjoy your Friends Society in London.

Having according to desire transmitted Your Salutations to Doctor Blair, was served with the inclosed Card, which is sent as he is pleased to direct: you [will] [2] perceive the great and anxious Concern about Dr Alex^r Munro Drummond, shall be very happy to enjoy as early satisfactory Accounts of him as consistent with Convenience, being with the truest respect

Dear Sir
Your most obed^t humble Servt
GPaton

Customhouse Edinburgh
    13 January 1775

[p. 2.] I took the Liberty of opening this Letter to say We are all well, I am glad Harry got safe to Town   adieu! [3]

A.P.

Address: The Reverend Dr Thomas Percy
        Easton Mauduit

---

[1] *Source:* British Museum, Add. MS. 32332, ff. 91–92.
[2] MS. torn.
[3] *Note in Mrs. Percy's hand.* The reference is to their son Henry (1763–83), scholar of Westminster School. She evidently forwarded the letter to her husband in London. (The letters "A.P." stand for Anne Percy.)

LXXXI
From Paton[1]

[March 25, 1775]

Dear Sir

The Reverend Dr Blair several Weeks ago obliged me with agreeable Accounts of your Arrival in London I hope now your Complaints are totally removed and that you enjoy a perfect State of Health as formerly, the continuation whereof is heartily wisht.

I take the Liberty by a Friend passing to London of informing you that the *Collector of the Scots Songs* &^{c} sent you last Winter is desirous to have your Sentiments of the Volume;[2] your Opinion of them with Advice how to arrange and what Remarks may be necessary will be most acceptable, as he has some thoughts during this present Vacation to set about reprinting the former Volume, which is entirely sold off and out of print to which he would incline the addition of this second Collection and make another Volume: I have reason to believe some discoveries have been made of similar Reliques, of which hope soon to be qualified to acquaint you particularly, when a Copy of these can be procured. It shall be my studious pleasure to serve you here whereof beg you will give me an opportunity in knowing what may be wanted, and oblige

Revd Dear Sir

Your most obedient and obliged

humble Servant GPaton

Customhouse Edinburgh
 25 March 1775

---

[1] *Source:* British Museum, Add. MS. 32332, f. 93. [2] See Letter LXVIII, p. 101.

LXXXII
From Paton[1]

[July 21, 1775]

Rev[d] Dear Sir

It is long since I had the pleasure of hearing from you: more engaging usefull attentions have employed you during that Interval.

I beg leave to inform you that M[r] Wotherspoon the Printer and assistant Collector of the *Scot's Songs* applied to me t'other day soliciting your favourable Return of the *M.SS. Volume of Songs* sent you last Year,[2] when he would be most singularly obliged for Communications of *Sir Richard Maitland's Scots Songs* or *any others* you will be kind enough as ornament the intended Publication with, as the Editors seem now resolved to begin and print off an Impression of these Poetical Pieces, this Autumn during the Recess of our Law Courts.

Be pleased to inform me if M[r] Gough returned to you *Sir David Lindsay's Satyres*[3] *4to* the defects of which Copy will be supplied (by your friendly pointing out) from the M.SS. Collection belonging to the Advocate's Liberary: when you are pleased to return them: and [p. 2.] am apt to believe Banantyne has interspersed more of this | *Knights Poems* in that Volume,[4] than may as yet have been published.

As you have canvassed several of *Jo. Major's short historical &c^a hints,* there's a passage lib. iv. Cap. 5. about David Earl of Huntington "iste est David de quo apud Gallos liber satis vulgaris loquitur, qui *de trium Regum filijs*[5] inscribitur, scilicet Franciæ, Angliæ et

---

[1] *Source:* British Museum, Add. MS. 32332, f. 94.

[2] See also Appendix I, p. 170.

[3] See Letter XLI, p. 60.

[4] There are no other poems by Lindsay in the Bannatyne MS.

[5] Paton secured a copy of the

French version of this work through Gough, who wrote to him (16 April 1776), "I have just got Le Livre des trois filz des roys de France, d'Angleterre et d'Ecosse which I believe is what Ld. Hailes enquired after. It is at his service. . . ." (National Li-

Scotiæ, et non differentem ab hoc in nostra lingua vernacula librum habemus."

L. Hailes is extremely anxious to have some Account of the Treatises here mentioned, but more especially that in the vulgar tongue: of this we can get no Information, should this have occurred to you, the communication will be most acceptable.

The favour of your Answer with Convenience will singular oblige

Revd Dear Sir

Your most obed^t humble Servt

GPaton

Customhouse Edinburgh
21 July 1775

Address: The Reverend Dr Thomas Percy

LXXXIII

From Percy[1]

London, 28 July, 1775.

Dear Sir

I am ashamed to think how long I had been indebted for a very kind Letter, when I was favoured with a second Mark of your most obliging attention. I hope you will pardon my silence, when I assure

brary of Scotland, MS. 29-5-6, Vol. I, n.f.) Hailes inserted a note on it in the 1779 edition of *Annals of Scotland*, Edinburgh, 2 vols., II, 341, "Corrections and Additions to Vol. I," and maintained that the version *"in nostra lingua vernacula"* was "fabulous." But an English version in manuscript did exist, though no copies of an early edition are known. See

The Three Kings' Sons (Englisht from the French). Edited from its *unique* MS. Harleian 326, about 1500 A.D. By F. J. Furnivall, 1895 (Early English Text Society, Extra Series, LXVII).

[1] *Source:* National Library of Scotland, MS. 29-5-8, Vol. I, f. 83; printed in Maidment, pp. 55–57.

you that for these three Months past I have been constantly chained down to the most disagreeable of all Situations, and what absorbs the attention the most of all other, the attendance on sick friends. The Duchess struggled for Life many weeks, and when Providence decided the Conflict most happily in her favour (and during that Conflict I was constantly down at Sion ² with her and continually [p. 2.] in her Antechamber) | the moment I could get a little respite I was both seized with a violent Illness myself, and have had the still greater Mortification of seeing a beloved Wife reduced twice to the point of death, who even at this moment lies deplorably ill and I fear in great danger.³ However I have roused myself up, and would not any longer defer writing. I have also sent away carriage paid this day, by the Edinburgh Waggon (which puts up at the Bird & Bush Edinburgh) a little Box containing (1) Bannatyne's MS. Collection of Scotish Poems. (2) The Volume of MS. Songs sent me last year. (3) A small Parcel for my Lord Hailes.

—Your little printed volume ⁴ in 4to intitled Sir David Lindsay's Satires, I have ventured to detain a little longer, till I can compare it [p. 3.] with a perfect Copy | transcribed from Bannatyne's MS. by Alan Ramsey,⁵ and lent me by his Son.—When I have examined it a little more I will send it you in a second Packet together with some of the Poems from Maitland, when I have had Leisure to consider them, which I have not had once since I received your last MS. Collection of Songs, and only glanced my eye cursorily over that Volume, which I have now returned; without having had time (from my other Avocations) to make the least use of the Contents. I hope now in the Course of next Winter to prepare a 4ᵗʰ Volume of Reliques ⁶ for the Press, and when I have selected some of Maitland's Poems for

² Sion House in Middlesex, a seat of the Dukes of Northumberland. A description of the house, with an illustration, is in Daniel Lysons's _Environs of London_, 1790, 4 vols., III, 90.

³ Mrs. Percy recovered, though her illness was long and severe.

⁴ Over "Collection" deleted.

⁵ See Letter LXVI, n. 3, p. 99, and Letter XLI, p. 59.

⁶ Percy gave up this project. See Letter CVII, p. 159, and Letter CVIII, n. 4, p. 162.

my own Work, I shall see what I can spare for your friend's Publication.

Should I any where meet with, or hear of the piece you mention [p. 4.] *De trium Regum Filiis* I shall not fail to give immediate Notice either to my Lord Hailes or to you.

I beg, Sir, you will present my most respectful thanks to the Gentlemen, who have so kindly indulged me with the long Loan of Bannatyne's MS. out of the Advocate's Library and to all who were instrumental in procuring me so great an Indulgence: and accept yourself the best thanks of

Dear Sir

Your most obliged

and faithful

Servant

T. Percy

PS/

Please to direct to me only at Northumberland House London without using any Inclosure.

LXXXIV

From Paton[1]

[August 7, 1775]

Revd Dear Sir

Your most courteous Favours of 28 Current reached me in due Course: too too sufficient are the Reasons of your Silence, but hope propitious Providence will remove the distresses of your noble connections and worthy Family by restoring both to good health again, which I sincerely pray may be soon.

I return you sincere Thanks for the Care taken in forwarding

[1] *Source:* British Museum, Add. MS. 32332, f. 97.

the two Manuscripts by Land, which shall be punctualy acknowledged how soon they are received: I have intimated to the Librarian that *Banantyne's M.SS.* is on it's return to this, making a Tender of your most gratefull Expressions for the indulged allowance of keeping it so long, which he promised to communicate to every one of the Faculty sharing in this Favour: these were cordially received.

It is quite proper and you are extremely welcome to retain *Sir David Lindsay's Satyres,* the more so as the Loan thereof in M.SS. transcribed by Mr Ramsay promises an opportunity of completing the printed Copy, which if could be easily done, I would most chearfully pay any Person you are pleased to employ to transcribe into the printed Book it's defects from this M.SS. belonging to Mr Ramsay if he will oblige me with this permission.

[p. 2.]   Your additional Volume will be most acceptable and deserves the highest as it must meet with due esteem from the Public, the regard designed our Country man Maitland will be properly valued, as it ought, here: Your benevolent attention to the proposed plan of reprinting the Scots Songs, with the generous hopes of gaining such a Treasure of Maitland's share from you gives the Publisher spirit, who desires me to present his most thankfull acknowledgements of Gratitude.

Your inclosed was forwarded: with the greatest respect

     I am
      Revd Dear Sir
       Your most obedient humble Servt
       GPaton

Custom^hs Edinburgh
 7 August 1775

 Address: The Reverend Dr Thomas Percy
   Northumberland house
   London

LXXXV
From Paton[1]

[September 1, 1775]

Revd Dear Sir

I now take the Liberty of inclosing your Receipt for *Bannantyne's Poems*, which was given to me on delivering the Book, which was done immediately after it's arrival here and how soon the Liberary was opened, at the same time got up your Order to Mr Davidson to whom I returned it, he desired acceptance of his Compliments, and Mr Brown this day presented me with the inclosed Letter also to be conveyed which I now do hoping all will reach you in safety.

It shall yield particular pleasure to learn that you are relieved from the distressfull apprehensions you lately labour'd under from the dangers threatned your most noble Patroness and beloved Spouse, sincerely wishing you every Comfort, I am

Revd Dear Sir
Your most obedient Servt
GPaton

Customhouse Edinburgh
1 September 1775

Address: The Reverend Dr Thomas Percy
Northumberland House
London

[*Enclosure* [2]]

Revd Sir

By the Hands of my good friend Mr Geo. Paton I have received Ballentyn's MS. Poems which you had in Loan from our Library

---

[1] *Source:* British Museum, Add. MS. 32332, f. 99. [2] *Source:* British Museum, Add. MS. 32332, f. 101.

And it is with great pleasure that I can add that the Book is not only in the same state of preservation in which it was when lent but is much improven by the additional references which you have taken the trouble to make in the Index.[3] I have delivered your Receipt to Mr Paton who will obligingly transmit it to you—You have the trouble of this note acknowledging the Receipt of the MS. from

Revd Sir

Your most obd^t humble Servt

Alexander Brown

Advocates' Library
1st Septr 1775

Address: To The Revd Dr Thomas Percy

LXXXVI

From Percy[1]

Northumberland House, Feb. 29. 1776

Dear Sir,

Tho' so long an Interval has intervened since any Letter has passed between us, do not think I can ever forget your many acts of friendship or that I should not be extremely concerned to lose your correspondence: Unfortunately I am so circumstanced, that amidst the multiplicity of other Letters, I am often driven to postpone those of my literary friends, till I find it difficult to resume the thread of the Correspondence: I hope however, you will permit me to reclaim it with *you* and be pleased to inform me how I can convey a Set of my ancient Poems to you, of which Dodsley has lately published a new Edition:[2] and tho' I have no share of the property of this Im-

[p. 2.] pression, I have | made Interest to procure a Copy for you.

---

[3] See *The Bannatyne Manuscript,* ed. Ritchie, I, xxvii.
[1] *Source:* National Library of Scot-land, MS. 29-5-8, Vol. I, f. 84;

printed in Maidment, pp. 57–59.
[2] The third edition of the *Reliques,* 1775, 3 vols.

—I am also ashamed in the highest degree to find that I have never paid a Bill for Books you bought for me the Summer before last: this discovery I only made 2 or 3 days ago, in turning over some Papers, when your bill stared me in the face: but as I have lost the memorandum, which you favoured me with informing where I could pay the money to your agent, or correspondent, I hope you will pardon the omission and give me a fresh Direction without delay. Any Letter for me, may be inclosed under Cover to His Grace the Duke of Northumberland at Northumberland House London: I should be most happy, if at the same time, you could employ me to execute | any Commission for you, as I really ³ feel myself under so [p. 3.] many obligations of this kind to you, that I long to discharge them by similar returns. I hope this will find you in perfect health: the readiness you have always shown to oblige me, leaves me no doubt but you will readily pardon my troubling you with the inclosed, to be delivered as directed. I am, Dear Sir, with increasing esteem

Your obliged and
faithful Servant
Thoˢ Percy

[*In Paton's hand.*]
£1.8.6 may be paid to Messʳˢ Richardson and Urquhart Booksellers ⁴ below the Exchange on Mʳ John Bell's Account.

LXXXVII
From Paton¹

[March 9, 1776]

Dear Sir

Your most acceptable Favours of 29ᵗʰ Ultimo came to hand this day and am extremely happy that our Correspondence is renewed,

---

³ MS. reads "I really I."
⁴ Richardson and Urquhart, book-sellers and publishers, Royal Exchange, London (*fl.* 1765–77).

¹ *Source:* British Museum, Add. MS. 32332, f. 103.

which shall be encouraged as fervently as possible on my part in chearfully complying on every Occasion with your requests.

Your Letter to Lord Hailes [2] was immediately conveyed to his Lordship, beg the same Channel may be used in any future time to any of your Correspondents.

I remember some time ago you wanted *Eginharti Vita Caroli magni* [3] *4to with the Print,* as it is some Months since this Edition fell into my hands and if you are not already provided with the Book, I must insist on your Acceptance of it, which shall be sent shortly in some Parcel for London—

I blush at your Generosity and am concerned to find you did put yourself to any trouble with M[r] Dodsley for a Copy of the last Edition of your valuable Poems, hope soon to hear that you are to oblige us with a fourth Volume, which you was so kind as inform me might be ready this Spring.

When convenient the Bill of £1·8·6 may be paid into Mess[rs] Richardson and Urquhart Booksellers below the Exchange London
[p. 2.] on Account of M[r] John Bell here, the | multiplicity of Correspondence is too substantial an apology and there is no cause to add more.

At present have no occasion to give you any trouble on my Account, beg acceptance of Thanks for the very kind Expressions on this head.

I have desired my Acquaintance M[r] Robertson [4] to call at Northumberland-house some time hence, when if it should suite your Convenience to let him have *Sir David Lindsay's Satyres,* provided

[2] See Percy-Hailes *Correspondence,* pp. 132–37, for this letter dated 29 February 1776.

[3] *Eginhartus de Vita et Gestis Caroli Magni, Trajecti ad Rhenum,* 1711, 4°. This edition has the portrait and genealogical table. See also Letter XVIII, p. 27.

[4] Robertson grew tired of these commissions. "I am sorry that M[r] Robertson is so untractable that when he came to M[r] Nichols for your Par-

cels, he said he was not a porter and refused to take them (Gough to Paton, 30 March 1793, National Library of Scotland, MS. 29-5-6, Vol. II, f. 76). Paton replied: "I never gave any offence, but rather promoted his advantage and welfare as far as lay in my power, but now it would seem he is ungratefull, so shall ever after despise him untill he amend his Conduct" (12 April 1793, MS. 29-5-7, Vol. II, n.f.).

you have done with it, as a particular friend here expresses an eager desire to see that Book, and doubts if ever any such was printed. Beg you will pardon the freedom used by inclosing this for him, which may be thrown into the pennypost.

It will ever afford me constant Joy to hear that You and Family are well being

Revd Dear Sir

Your most obedient and obliged

humble Servt   GPaton

Customhouse Edinburgh
9 March 1776

LXXXVIII

From Paton[1]

[March 12, 1776]

Dear Sir

This day Lord Hailes sent me the inclosed[2] soliciting that I would transmit it to you, as his Lordship was uncertain at the time of your Address.

I hope this Week to have an opportunity in a Parcel for London to forward *Eginharti Vita Caroli* 4to as promised in my last, of which beg your Acceptance, hoping you will excuse the freedom used a post or two ago of troubling you with a Letter to a Friend in Westminster.

I ever am

Revd Dear Sir

Your most obedient and obliged

humble Servt   GPaton

[1] *Source:* British Museum, Add. MS. 32332, f. 104.

[2] Probably an acknowledgement of Percy's long note on the death of Malcolm III, which Percy had sent to Hailes in his letter of 29 February (see Letter LXXXVII, n. 2, p. 128). Hailes printed the note in the first volume of his *Annals of Scotland*.

Customhouse Edinburgh
    12 March 1776

Address: The Reverend Dr Percy
        Northumberland House
        London

Docket: Mr Paton 1776

LXXXIX

From Paton[1]

[March 26, 1776]

Revd Dear Sir

A worthy good Friend[2] of mine in Orkney in the Course of his researching thro' these Islands was served with the inclosed Verses from a Country man, which is thought to be co-eval or older than Shakespear, the original as written by the Man I send you, if worthy of notice, your thoughts on it.

The same Gentleman informs me that he has a *Norn Song* or Ballat[3] in that Language as repeated to him some Years ago by an aged Inhabitant of the Island of *Foula,* who could neither read nor

[1] *Source:* British Museum, Add. MS. 32332, f. 106.

[2] Rev. George Low (1747–95), minister of Birsay, Orkney, naturalist and antiquary. See the *D.N.B.*

[3] A letter from Low to Paton (27 February 1776) reads: "I lately had from a young man the enclosed Ballad, written from his memory. It looks like antique, and if genuine and not published might be acceptable to Dr. Piercy, on account of Shake-speare's play founded on the same subject, perhaps on the ballad or vice versa. He was not master of Spelling it truely and I think it would be better in four Line Stanzas." (National Library of Scotland, MS. 29-5-8, Vol. III, f. 81; printed in *A Tour Through the Islands of Orkney and Schetland,* by George Low, ed. W. Pearce, introduction by Joseph Anderson, Kirkwall, 1879, p. lvi.)

write, but enjoyed a most tenacious memory, altho' he is no adept in that Language he copied it while the aged peasant repeated it; [4] he expresses an earnest desire that it be communicated to you for an Explanation, whereof if agreeable I shall order a Copy to be transmitted here, which will in Course convey it to you at London or wherever you are pleased to instruct me.

> I ever am
> Revd Dear Sir
> Your most obedient and obliged humble Servant
> GPaton

Customhouse Edinburgh
26 March 1776

PS. I am just now informed the second Edition of the *Scots Songs* is printing,[5] when a Volume is ready it shall be sent you.

Address: The Reverend Dr Thomas Percy
Northumberland house
London

XC
From Percy[1]

> Northumb^d House, April
> 23^d 1776.

Dear Sir,

I received your very obliging Letter and the Copy of the old ballad for which be pleased to accept my grateful thanks: I have not

---

[4] See Low's account, *op. cit.*, pp. 107–14, Letter XCVII, p. 142, and Letter C, p. 146.

[5] It appeared in April.

[1] *Source:* National Library of Scotland, MS. 29-5-8, Vol. I, f. 85; printed in Maidment, pp. 59–60.

received Eginhart's Life of Charlemagne which you mention, nor is it at all necessary.—I have taken the Liberty to send a Copy of the new Edition of the Reliques &c. by Mr James Robertson, and hope you will accept them, as a small Token for the present, of that regard with which I am   Dear Sir
                              Your much obliged Servant
                              Thos Percy

Address: To Mr Geo. Paton
           at the Custom house
           Edinburgh

XCI
From Paton[1]

[May 13, 1776]

Dear Sir

Your most acceptable Favours came to hand some days ago of date 23^d past. I am ashamed of your trouble taken in puting into Mr Robertson's hands the new Edition of the *Reliques* &c^a which he wrote me will now be on its way here.

I hope the Life of Charlemagne will by this time be sent you, our late unfavourable weather has undoubtedly retarded the parcel reaching London.

The days of the publisher[2] was prolonged just to publish a new Edition of the *Scots Songs 2 Vol. with a hasty Glossary,* a Copy whereof awaits you, and should be glad to know, whether I may transmit it to London, or Alnwick Castle, to the later of which places you may shortly be removing.

[1] *Source:* British Museum, Add. MS. 32332, ff. 108–09.
[2] John Wotherspoon died 3 May 1776; buried in Greyfriars Churchyard, Edinburgh.

How soon the *Norn Ballad* or *Poem* appears I will forward it.

D[r] Cuming [3] of Dorchester is extremely anxious that a *Dictionary of our Scots Langage* should be set about and that immediately as he justly observes that | it is almost *evanescent*, this must be a labour [p. 2.] of much time and application, which cannot be confined to the industrious Collection of one Person as both learned and unlearned can offer a mite here:

I heartily wish to fall in with one to arrange properly your most excellent *Glossaries*, intermixing these of Gawin Douglas,[4] Ray,[5] L[d] Hailes [6] &[ca] &[ca] and fairly transcribed to which may be added many local words, when thus collected. I might procure a printer to make an Impression of an hundred Copies to disperse [7] properly amongst the carefull and Ingenious [8] here in our various shires and elsewhere for their varieties, after which the different Explanations &c might be collected and if possible the Etymologies also. I will rejoice in having your countenance in this, with what directions you would be pleased to communicate to further such a Scheme. I shall most chearfully contribute and when once disengaged from a piece of business, which will occupy all this Summer, I will do all in my power to forward this plan under your auspicious regulations.

I understand that you desired a further | perusal of *Sir David* [p. 3.] *Lindsay's Satyres*, which reached me in great safety, as I have got

---

[3] William Cuming (1714–88), educated at the High School and University of Edinburgh (M.D.1752) and at Paris and Leyden. He settled at Dorchester in 1738; he became a Fellow of the Society of Antiquaries in 1769. See an account of him in *The Gentleman's Magazine*, 1788, I, 364.

[4] See Letter XLIX, n. 8, p. 72.

[5] John Ray (1627–1705), Fellow of the Royal Society, author of *A Collection of English Words not generally used*, 1674, 8°, and *A Collection of English Proverbs*, Cambridge, 1670, 8°. Augmented editions were frequent until 1817.

[6] The glossary to Hailes's *Ancient Scottish Poems*, Edinburgh, 1770. Hailes's interest in glossaries, which began with his *Specimen of a Book*, 1765, continued throughout his life. His MS. drafts and notes are preserved at Newhailes (MSS. 443, 444, and 470).

[7] MS. reads "dispress."

[8] Distributing specimen glossaries was a common practice. Copies of those sent out by Hailes are preserved in the National Library of Scotland, MS. 3565, and at Newhailes. See also the Introduction, pp. vii and viii.

nothing added to it hitherto and the present use of it being nigh over for this Season: please let me know when and how it may be conveyed to you again, at the same time plead to be excused for so hastily requesting it here. I ever am

Revd Dear Sir

Your most obed^t and obliged

humble Ser^t   GPaton

Customhouse Edinb^r

    13 May 1776

     Address: The Reverend Dr Thomas Percy

        Northumberland House

        London

XCII

From Percy[1]

Easton Mauduit, Feb.5.1777

Dear Sir,

    I have so often trespassed upon your good-nature by long Intervals of Silence, and you have so constantly extended your pardon to me, that I am not altogether without hope of your indulgent Forgiveness at present, tho I have so little right to expect it. The truth is I am often so idle, and so busy, that one while I have no leisure to write to my friends; and at other times no Ability:[2] which tho' no good excuse, yet is an ingenuous confession: and at least exempts me from one Imputation, which would be unpardonable, that of disregard, or Disrespect. Neither of these can ever be the case with

---

[1] *Source:* National Library of Scotland, MS. 29-5-8, Vol. I, f. 86; printed in Maidment, pp. 60–63.

[2] Over "Inclination" deleted.

regard to Mr Paton, to whose Friendship | I have been and am so [p. 2.] continually obliged.—To your kind attention, I believe, I have been lately indebted for two Edinburgh Catalogues; for which be pleased to accept my best thanks. One came inclosed in Covers to the Duke; but as his Grace was then in Cornwall and I in Northamptonshire, I never received it, till the Auction was over. As it frequently happens, that the Duke and I are separated far asunder, which occasions great Inconvenience in the transmitting of Packets, I must particularly intreat, (as I think I did once before) that you would be pleased never to send me anything more, than a single Letter, under the Duke's Covers. I had rather pay ten times the Postage or carriage than trouble his Grace with my Packets when we are absent from each other.—But it is expected that all franking will be suppressed.[3]

I have since received J. Bell's Catalogue for 1777: this was left [p. 3.] for me at Northumberland House, and I imagine came from you: Will you have the goodness to secure (and send by the Waggon directed to me at Northumberland House) the following Articles.[4] viz

	N°			
Fol°	86.	Froissart &c.	18^s	
	395.	Diodorus &c.	7^s	1:8:6
8vo	2320.	Vida &c.	1^s	
	2887.	Gibbon's essay &c.	2^s 6^d	

The money I will pay to Messrs Richardson and Urquhart or to whomsoever else you please. (By the bye, I hope you received the last payment which I made there last year.)—I should be happy (tho' I so little deserve it) to receive the favour of a Line and to hear what ingenious Works are going forward under your Auspices. Be please[d] to inclose to me under Cover (To the Earl of Sussex

---

[3] Stricter regulations were not enforced till 1837. Franking ceased with the introduction of the Penny Post in 1840. See Percy-Evans *Correspondence*, p. 89, n. 11.

[4] It has not been possible to identify the editions.

at Easton Mauduit, near Castle Ashby, in Northamptonshire) with a *P* in a Corner of the Direction for Distinction.—

I am with great Esteem and Regard,

Dear Sir

Your most obliged Servant

T. Percy

[p. 4.] PS/

I should have written to you in the Autumn but all my attention was then and has been ever since ingrossed by the fatal Illness and subsequent Death of the Duchess of Northumberland,[5] which has engaged me ever since in constant business. You told me last Spring there was a New Edition of the Scots Songs [6] in 2 Vol[s]. does it contain any Improvements?—You also hoped to procure a Norn Song. Have you succeeded? Pray could you inform me, who are Executors of M[r] Foulis [7] of Glasgow?

XCIII

From Paton[1]

[February 15, 1777]

Rev[d] Dear Sir

I was agreeably favored with yours of 5th Current the Excuse of silence is sufficient, it will at all times give me pleasant sensations to know that D[r] Percy is well: the late Death of Her Grace the Duchess of Northumberland must have involved you into a flood of business, concern with other varieties, that I sincerely feel for your Loss.

---

[5] She died 5 December 1776.

[6] See Letter XCI, p. 132.

[7] Robert Foulis (b. 1707), brother and partner of Andrew Foulis (1721–75), died in 1776. His son Andrew succeeded to the business. See Letter XCIII, n. 3, p. 137.

[1] *Source:* British Museum, Add. MS. 32332, ff. 110–11.

The directions about your Address shall be punctualy observed and none other used untill favored with other restrictions, of which when convenient.

Mr Bell has duly credited you for the payment made to Messrs Richardson and Urquhart, but am sorry to inform that all the Books of your present order are long since disposed of: N° 2320 Vida &^c was the same Book and but a part, as inserted in his former Catalogue, it is now sold.

Nothing worthy of any notice is presently carrying on here, neither do hear of any soon intended.

Our Bookseller[s] here, when any remarkable Collection of Books occurr, take the opportunity, by the Stage from this to London, of sending a parcel of Catalogues to one of their correspondents, who agreeable to their directions forward one to any particular Gentleman in the City and in this Line you have been served with Mr Bell's.

The Publisher of the *Scot's Songs 2 Vol 12°* just enjoyed Life as [p. 2.] hastily to conclude the Book; since his Death the Sale has been more numerous than expectation, as I have some few Articles for my Friend Mr Gough, but cannot have them earlier than middle of nixt month; with these a Copy shall be left for your Acceptance at Northumberland house, from whence hope it will find conveyance.

My worthy Acquaintance a Clergyman in Orkney [2] has had of late his largest portion of affliction, by the deaths of his Spouse and only Child, that I must readylie grant him pardon for omitting to send me *Norn Song,* however as I write him soon will request his sending it up or at least solicite the bringing it here, as it would be salutary to retire from the place of his Grief for a time, that variety might administrate some relief. You may be assured of it's being sent you how soon it comes to my hands.

Mr Robert Foulis left a Son,[3] who I presume may carry on busi-

---

[2] Letter LXXXIX, n. 2, p. 130, and Letter XCI, p. 133.

[3] Andrew Foulis, the younger (1758?–1829), succeeded to the busi- ness, which was insolvent. He remained University Printer till 1796. Thereafter his livelihood became precarious, and he died in poverty. See

ness, he is unknown to me, suppose is young and must require years of experience to execute work similar to his Father and Uncle the latter of whom Mr Andrew managed the operations with diligent precision and exactness: I cannot affirm whether he is continued University Bookseller and Printer.

Dr Patrick Cuming's [4] Books are presently on Sale these are only [p. 3.] a part of his Collection, part of which | in his Life time were disposed of having moved to a house where he had not convenience to arrange them, amongst them are several scarce Articles, a Copy of this Catalogue am pretty certain would be left for you at His Grace's House London.

I shall always esteem it a favor to be any how assisting in answering your requests, being

Dear Sir

Your most obed^t humble

Servt GPaton

Customhouse Edinburgh

15 Februry 1777   Answ^d 26 April 1777 *[In Percy's hand]*

XCIV

From Percy[1]

Northumb^d House April 26th 1777

Dear Sir,

Having an opportunity of inclosing this under a Frank to Dr Blair, I gladly seize the Pen. I was favoured with yours of the 15th of Feb.

The Glasgow University Press 1638–1931, by James MacLehose, Glasgow, 1931, pp. 195–203.
[4] Patrick Cumin or Cuming, D.D. (1695–1776), minister of the Old Kirk Parish, Edinburgh, from 1732,

and Professor of Church History in Edinburgh University, 1737–62. He was a leader of the Moderate party.
[1] *Source:* National Library of Scotland, MS. 29-5-8, Vol. I, f. 87.

and should have acknowledged it before, but I have laboured under very ill health a great part of the time since I received it. I sincerely wish and hope that you may have been more fortunate in this respect. In your last you are so good, as to mention that a Copy of the *Scots Songs 2 vol.* 12° would be left for me about the middle of march, as you intended to forward | them in a parcel to Mr Gough: As I have [p. 2.] not seen him lately to inquire if he has received them, I just mention it lest there should have been any miscarriage: but you have obliged too much with your former favours, for me to be so unreasonable as to desire more on the same terms. Be assured that I must ever esteem myself

Dear Sir
Your most obliged
Humble Servant
Thos Percy

Address: To Geo. Paton Esq
     at the Custom house
     Edinburgh.

XCV

From Paton[1]

[May 1, 1777]

Dear Sir

I am this day favoured with yours of 26th ultimo, expressing the valetudinary State you have been in for some time but hope is now removed, that your wonted health is restored, it's my sincere desire that this may find you in such a State.

The Collection of Scot's Songs 2 Vol. has been long by me for transmission to you for acceptance, our Printers here being so dilatory

---

[1] *Source:* British Museum, Add. MS. 32332, f. 112.

in finishing a small Article, which I promised to Mr Gough, this expect may be ready in a Week or two hence when the Book will be forwarded in a Parcel to an Acquaintance in London whom I shall tender injunctions to deliver it into Northumberland house for you [p. 2.] hoping | for your Indulgence till this makes it's approach to you. I ever am   Dear Sir

                    Your most obedient and
                    obliged humble Servant
                    GPaton

Customhouse Edinburgh
    1 May 1777

    Address: The Reverend Dr Thomas Percy
            Northumberland house
            London

XCVI

From Percy[1]

Northumberland House, May 22^d 1777

Dear Sir,

You have been so particularly obliging upon all occasions, that I flatter myself you will excuse my requesting the favour of you to procure a Copy of the Sermon here advertised, viz.

Just published. Price 6d. | And sold by *William Shaw* and *William Creech,* Edinburgh, and *Peter* | *Tait* Bookseller, Glasgow; | *The Dominion of Providence over the Passions of Men:* | A SERMON, Preached at Princetown, on the 17th of May. 1776, | Being the

[1] *Source:* National Library of Scotland, MS. 29-5-8, Vol. I, f. 88;   printed in Maidment, pp. 63–64.

General Fast appointed by the Congress through the United | Colonies. | To which is added, | An ADDRESS to the Natives of Scotland residing in America. | by JOHN WITHERSPOON, D.D. President of the College of New Jersey, formerly Minister in Paisley. | It is not the intention of the Editors of the present edition of the | Doctor's Sermon and address, to gain friends to his sentiments—this | is not likely to be the case with any who will peruse them with attention; | but to show what artful means, and fallacious arguments have been made | use of by ambitious and self-designing men, to stir up the poor infatuated Americans to the present rebellious measures; what an active hand even | Dr. Witherspoon has had therein; and to convince his friends in this | country of the truth of his being a chief promoter of the American revolt.[2]

and be pleased to send it in one or more Covers directed to *the Revd Mr Lort*[3] under an Inclosure—To the Lord Bishop of Chester[4] at Lambeth near London.

I have a further Favour to request of you, that you will honour [p. 2.] with your acceptance the 2 Vol^s of Capt. Cooke's[5] Voyage, which my Bookseller had orders to send you last Monday (Carriage Paid; which I mention only lest you should be charged twice.)—I desired him to get good Impressions of the plates and hope you will admit them into your Library, as a small tribute of that respect with which I am

Dear Sir

Your very faithful

and obliged Servant

Thos Percy

---

[2] A cutting of the printed advertisement. This celebrated sermon, first published at Philadelphia in 1776, was attacked in the *Weekly Magazine, or Edinburgh Amusement* on 14 March, 24 April, 1 May and 19 June 1777 in articles from Paisley signed W. C.

[3] Michael Lort (1725–90), Regius Professor of Greek at Cambridge, 1759–71. For Percy's correspondence with him (1781–90), see Nichols's *Illustrations*, VII, 438–517.

[4] Beilby Porteus (1731–1808), successively Bishop of Chester (from 1776) and of London (from 1787).

[5] *A Voyage towards the South Pole and round the World . . . in the Years 1772–75, written by James Cook, Commander of the Resolution,* 1777, 4°, 2 vols.

XCVII

From Paton[1]

[May 26, 1777]

Dear Sir

I am favoured this day with yours of 22ᵈ Current and have in obedience thereto sent to the Revᵈ Mʳ Lort *Witherspoon's Sermon.*

An Acquaintance purposes this Week seting out for London, who will leave *the Collection of Scot's Songs 2 Vol. 12°* for you at Northumberland house.

The Orkney Clergyman, who promised me the Norse Song or Poem, has been daylie expected here for some weeks past is not come to Town yet, but the moment he arrives and serves me with it I will accept of the first opportunity by Post to have it conveyed to your hands.

Your Liberality of ordering me Capᵗ Cooke's Voyage puts me out of Countenance; any article from you is most acceptable, but blush at the expence laid out for so valueable a performance, which I see is [p. 2.] arrived in Town: I beg you to | name anything from this Country that would be any way worthy your accepting, which will yield a sensible pleasure to be conveyed you by

Dear Sir

Your most obedient and most

obliged humble

Servant GPaton

Customhouse Edinburgh
    26 May 1777

Address: The Reverend Dʳ Thomas Percy
        Northumberlandhouse
        London

[1] *Source:* British Museum, Add. MS. 32332, f. 114.

XCVIII

From Percy[1]

Northumberland House June 14. 1777

Dear Sir,

Accept my best thanks for your ready compliance with my former request; which like other favours too readily granted, only brings fresh trouble upon yourself. I must once more beg leave to apply to you to send *two* more copies of Dr Witherspoon's Sermon, to the Bishop of Chester: be pleased to send them by different Posts, and even in more Covers[2] than 2 or 3, if there should be any danger of their exceeding, each, the weight of 2 ounces.

The Sermons need no other Direction but, To The Lord Bishop [p. 2.] of Chester at Lambeth near London: and require no internal Cover. At the same time I should be glad to be favoured with a Line from you, addressed to me under Cover To His Grace the Duke of Northumberland, at Northumberland House London; in which I should be glad if you would give me some Account of this Dr Witherspoon whose character and history are little known at this end of the Island: tho' I conclude he has made a noise in North-Britain as well as New England, &c.

I suppose your Friend is not yet come to London with the Col- [p. 3.] lection of Songs, &c. but I beg you will not be anxious about it, I have already received too many favours of that sort from you, to have the least Right to be urgent for fresh ones.

Adieu! my Dear Sir, and
believe me to be
Your most obliged
Humble Servant
Thos Percy

---

[1] *Source:* National Library of Scotland, MS. 29-5-8, Vol. I, f. 89; printed in Maidment, pp. 65–69.

[2] Over "packets" deleted.

[p. 4.] PS/
Lord Percy,[3] who is arrived safe and well, gives us hope that the
War will be terminated in the ensuing Campagne.

XCIX

From Paton[1]

[June 20, 1777]

Rev[d] Dear Sir

As you requested I have dispatched two Copies of D[r] Witherspoon's Sermons to Lambeth under the Address of Lord Bishop of
Chester by former and this Post and shall be ready on all occasions
to comply with your orders as may be communicated.

D[r] Witherspoon[2] is son of the late Rev[d] M[r] James Witherspoon[3] Minister at Yester about 20 miles or thereby South east of
Edinburgh a well bred Gentleman universaly esteemed and particularly caressed by his Patron the Marquis of Tweedale[4] of very
moderate principles: the Son was educated at this University very
shrewd, has great abilities tho' not always applied to the best purposes,
he was soon settled in a Country Parish in the Shire of Air where
he commenced very rigid in his principles and by that means obtained
a high esteem amongst his followers, which were numerous, many

[3] Hugh, Earl Percy (1742–1817),
became the second Duke. He served
as a major general in the British army.
He had embarked for Boston in the
spring of 1774 and took part in several actions around that city. After a
dispute with his superior, Lord Howe,
he demanded and obtained a recall.

[1] *Source:* British Museum, Add.
MS. 32332, f. 116.

[2] John Witherspoon (1722–94),
D.D., St. Andrews, 1764; minister at

Beith, Ayrshire, 1745–57, and at
Paisley (Laigh Kirk) from 1757 to
1768 when he left for America and
was elected President of Princeton College in New Jersey in 1768. See *President Witherspoon, A Biography,* by
Varnum Lansing Collins, Princeton,
1925.

[3] James Witherspoon (1691–1759),
minister at Yester in East Lothian.

[4] John Hay, fourth Marquis of
Tweeddale (*c.* 1695–1762).

years ago he published a very | unworthy Pamphlet intitled "Ec- [p. 2.]
clesiastical Characteristicks" [5] a Satyre on many of his Brethern the
Clergy, which ran thro' two or more Editions and was again collected amongst his other Tracts and Sermons and republished by
Dilly [6] at London (I think) in 3 Volumes 12°. he always possessed a
large share of Ambition so obtained a Transportation to the Charge
of Paisley near Glasgow, where his Collegue M[r] Bain [7] and he
differ'd, the former in disgust quitted his Kirk and commenced a
Sectary having opened a meeting house in this place; shortly after
the Doctor's having had some disputes with some of his hearers, for
which he was prosecuted before a civil Court and has not very long
since been cost the fine and Expences thereof is supposed to have cost
him or his Sureties (for such he was obliged to find before he quitted
Scotland) about or above £500.[8] Several Years ago he accepted of
an Invitation to America where he had been much caressed by people
of his own principles and actualy sate a Member of that rebellious
Cabal the Congress; [9] having some Lands | there which he wanted [p. 3.]

[5] *Ecclesiastical Characteristics, or the Arcana of Church Policy, being an Attempt to open up the Mystery of Moderation,* Glasgow, 1753, 8°, fifth edition, Edinburgh, 1763, 8°. It attacked the dominant Moderate party in the Church of Scotland, whose measures were considered tyrannical.

[6] Paton refers to *Essays on Important Subjects,* published by Dilly in 1765, 12°, 3 vols. The first edition of Witherspoon's collected *Works* appeared at Philadelphia, 1800–01, 4 vols., 8°.

[7] James Baine (1710–90), minister at Paisley (High Kirk), 1756–66. Baine thought the policy of the Church of Scotland Erastian and therefore seceded in 1766 to become minister of the Relief Chapel in Nicolson's Park in a south suburb of Edinburgh. He published *Memoirs of Modern Church Reformation; or, the*

History of the General Assembly 1766, Edinburgh, 1766, 8°, which gave a full statement of his position. See also an account in *Annals of the General Assembly of the Church of Scotland from the Origin of the Relief in 1752, to the Rejection of the Overture on Schism in 1766,* Edinburgh, 1840, pp. 313–29.

[8] This account is unfair to Witherspoon. In 1762 he published a sermon entitled *Sinners sitting in the Seat of the Scornful: Seasonable Advice to Young Persons.* (See *Works,* 1815, V, 90–125.) In the preface, he rebuked by name some young men who had been guilty of profane behavior. An action for damages was brought against him and the case dragged on till 1776, when he was ordered in absence to pay £150 damages. He had many sympathizers.

[9] In 1776 he was chosen representa-

to improve he schemed that destructive plan of Emigration [10] from this Country wherein he and his Emissary Mr John Pagan Merchant in Glasgow were pretty successfull in aluring many poor Highlanders to that Country where numbers of them perished either during the Voyage or for want when they reached America. his desire of Money is equal with his thirst of Ambition and both seem to be his passionate favorites: had his turn been properly applied he would have made an eminent figure. I remember him well, of a gloomy countenance and scarcely could ever look one fully in the face: he is still much esteemed amongst the Enthusiastical Class in this Country.—Thus have I given you the outlines of this Trumpeter of Rebellion and sure I am, had his Father been alive, at this time, from my personal knowledge of that Gentleman, he would have abhorred and even punished the Son for his behaviour.

I am

Dear Sir

Your most obed^t and obliged

humble Servt

GPaton

Customhouse Edinburgh
20 June 1777

C

From Paton[1]

[August 27, 1777]

Revd Dear Sir

Being lately unexpectedly most agreeably surprised with a visit from my Friend in Orkney, having remained here only a few days,

tive for New Jersey in the general congress.

[10] This scheme provoked much controversy, especially in Britain, but was not discreditable to Witherspoon. See *President Witherspoon*, I, 149–56.

[1] *Source:* Bodleian Library, MS. Percy, C. 1, ff. 60–61.

he allowed me to copy the inclosed *Norn Ballad*[2] from his Notes during his Journey thro' these Islands of Orkney and Schetland, which if acceptable to his Friends in England possibly these may be some time hence ushered into the public.

This was repeated to him by a very old man *William Henry* a Farmer in the Island of *Foula* (he believes since dead) who neither could read nor write so disqualified to either direct the genuine writing or pronouncing of The Language, as it was taken down while he repeated the Song, the general History he gave of it was this: "An Earl of Orkney while rambling on the Coast of Norway saw and fell in Love with *Hildina* the King's daughter, her passion being reciprocal he carried her off during her Father's Absence, who was engaged in War at that time with some of his neighbours: on his return home he pursued them with an Army to Orkney, his daughter advising her Husband the Earl to make offers of submission &ᶜ which seemingly being accepted of by the King of Norway, he was afterwards changed in his mind by the artifices of his Courtier *Hiluge*, who formerly entertained hopes of marrying the Lady; at last the dispute ended in Blows and the Earl was killed by *Hiluge* who cut off his Head and then threw it at his Spouse Hildina being obliged to return with her Father to Norway: where a little time after Hiluge makes a demand of her as his Wife from the King, which she is persuaded to by her Father; who at the Nuptial Ceremony requests to be permitted to fill the Wine, this being obtained, Hildina infused therein a drug which overpowered the Company into a dead Sleep, from whence she caused convey her Father safely and then set the House on fire, *Hiluge* perishing in the Flames unpitied and in revenge for the Cruelty expressed to her at the Death of her Husband the Earl of Orkney."[3] Thus far Tradition instructed the old Man to repeat, but whether founded on any real Fact is dubious. Mʳ Low

[2] Paton's transcript is in the Bodleian Library, MS. Percy, C. 1, ff. 62–64. See Letter LXXXIX, p. 130. Another version with variants is printed in George Barry's *History of the* *Orkney Islands*, Edinburgh, 1805, Appendix X, pp. 484–90.

[3] The story is based on the *Sörlathattr*. See *The Orkneyinga Saga*, ed. Joseph Anderson, Edinburgh, 1873, 8°, pp. cxiii–cxv.

said he was the only person he met with could speak the Norn Language [4] so fluently as to converse in it, in this Island: a benevolent, rational country man adding that he mentioned three Kinds of Poetry sung by the old Men in Norn, the *Vysie* or *Vyse* the Heroic repeated by the fireside in Winter: the 2ᵈ used at public meetings, now only to the dance, and the 3ᵈ at both.[5]

I have lately heard of a Collection of Danish Poems intitled *Kempe vice*,[6] which is said to signifie *Heroic Actions*, containing an History of all the Norn and Danish Invasions in Britain,—probably this Orkney Ballad may be inserted amongst them but having no opportunity of learning more about this Book I can give no further account of its contents being quite unacquainted with that northern language, if in the course of a future inquiry this Book can be procured from the [p. 2.] Continent | you shall hear of it, or should I be fortunate enough to gain a Copy or two, your acceptance of it will be a favour done me but possibly this is well known to you: a Gentleman in this Country, who mentioned it to me exprest a fondness to have it translated into the British language as it possibly might throw some light on the ancient history of this Country altho' interwoven with Fable.

I hope the Collection of *Scot's Songs* left at Northumberland House have reached you before this time, when *Ferguson's Poems* [7] appear these shall be forwarded: a most incorrect miserable Copy of Sir D. Lindsay's Poems [8] was lately reprinted here, so very basely executed with such a number of ommissions &ᶜ that I think shame to

---

[4] Orkney Norn was dying out by the eighteenth century. See Hugh Marwick, *The Orkney Norn*, Oxford, 1929, 8⁰, p. xxvi.

[5] Paton is confused; Low's statement is: ". . . he spoke of three kinds of poetry used in Norn, and repeated or sung by the old men; the Ballad (or Romance, I suppose); the Vysie or Vyse, now commonly sung to dances; and the simple Song. By the account he gave of the matter, the first seems to have been valued here chiefly for its subject, and was commonly repeated in winter by the fireside; the second seems to have been used in publick meetings, now only sung to the dance; and the third at both." See *A Tour Through the Islands of Orkney and Schetland*, p. 107.

[6] An edition of the Danish Kempeviser or Kjaempeviser was published by Peder Syv in Copenhagen, 1695.

[7] See Letter XXXVII, n. 2, p. 53.

[8] *The Works of the Famous and Worthy Knight, Sir David Lindsay of the Mount*, Edinburgh, 1776–77, 2 vols.

transmitt it, as I should fondly hope some time soon hence a more complete copy of his works may be undertaken by a correct hand.[9]

Nothing of any consequence is carrying on here at the time: I shall be happy to be any how serviceable in this Country, being

Revd Dear Sir

Your most obed^t and obliged

humble Servt   GPaton

Customhouse Edinburgh

    27 August 1777

PS. If the Ballad is intelligible a Translation thereof would be acceptable to the Collector the Revd Mr Low [10] to be inserted in his *Journal* &^c

GP

CI

From Percy[1]

Alnwick Castle, Aug. 29th 1777.

Dear Sir

I was preparing to thank you for your most obliging Present of the Scotish Ballads in 2 Volumes which followed me to this Place; when I received the additional Favour of your very kind Letter, inclosing the Norn Song: The Language is unknown to me: and as I

---

[9] The next edition of Lindsay's *Works* was by George Chalmers, 1806, 8°, 3 vols.

[10] Low says, "A literal translation . . . I could not procure, but the substance is this." Then follows the account that is given by Paton in this letter. See *A Tour Through* . . .

Orkney and Schetland, p. 113. For an elucidation of the language of the ballad, see *Hildinakvadet*, by Marius Hægstad, Christiania, 1900.

[1] *Source:* National Library of Scotland, MS. 29-5-8, Vol. I, f. 90; printed in Maidment, pp. 69–72.

find from your Account that it is equally so to Mr Low, who wrote it down from the Mouth of the Reciter, I think it a great Pity, that he [p. 2.] did not write down a Translation of | it (which should have been as literal as possible) from the Mouth of the old Orkney Farmer, who gave it him from Memory.—However tho' he be dead and tho' none of his Countrymen can speak the Norn familiarly, probably some old Persons may be found, who can understand it when repeated. After all, if Mr Low should publish any Account of the Orkneys,[2] I hope he will not fail to print this Song, which is perhaps the [p. 3.] only specimen now extant | of the Poetry of those Islands. However that may be, I beg you will believe that for this and all your kind favours I remain

Dear Sir
Your most obliged
& faithful Servant
Thos Percy

PS/
            I am now returning for some months to come, into Northampton-
[p. 4.] shire, where a Line will always reach me | directed under Cover To The Earl of Sussex at Easton Mauduit (by Bozeate Bag) near Wellingboro' Northamptonshire. And remember to insert the P for distinction.

---

[2] Low was disappointed in his efforts to have his varied MSS. published. They were freely used by other naturalists and antiquaries. The Tour did not appear till 1879 (See Letter LXXXIX, n. 3, p. 130). Part of a MS., long missing, of Low's Tour through the North Isles of Ork- ney was printed in the Old Lore Miscellany for July, 1915. Part of another MS., A Description of Orkney (1773), was published by Hugh Marwick in Proceedings of the Orkney Antiquarian Society, Kirkwall, 1924, II, 49–58 and Introduction, p. xii.

CII
From Paton[1]

[September 6, 1777]

Reverend Dear Sir

Some days ago I was obliged with your most agreeable Favours assuring that the triffle of Scot's Songs had come to hand, as also the *Norn Ballad,* which I did suspect might prove unintelligible, however Mr Low shall be solicited to use every endeavour to get a Translation of it if any of the Farmer's Family can supply this desired defect, tho' it is doubted whether any of the Inhabitants of the Island of *Foula* (where it was recited to him from Memory) now can perform the Task. Your request of having it inserted into his Description &^c of Orkney and Schetland if *printed,* shall be insisted on; and prior to that, a Copy of it (tho' not so distinctly written as the one sent you) being left with me I intend putting into the Hands of a Gentleman who resided long in that Country and now settled here, for his explanation of it, which when obtained you may depend on my Conveyance to you.

I am very well assured that there is a Collection of *Old Songs* and *Historical Ballads* under the Title of *Kempe Vice,*[2] unknown in this Country, a copy of which I have some hopes of procuring from Denmark or Norway thro' the inquiry of severals[3] to whom addresses have been made to pick up this Book consisting of 300 or more Songs mostly relating to the Danish Invasions of Britain, for which purpose I have solicited a friend at Hamburgh to make the same search for it, possibly this Song may make one of the Number but if this Book shall fall to my Lot, the same shall be as quickly forwarded to you as opportunity may present, altho' it is scarcely hoped for till the Spring

[1] *Source:* Bodleian Library, MS. Percy, C. 1, f. 65.
[2] See Letter C, n. 6, p. 148.
[3] For this usage, see *O.E.D.*, VIII, 570, 3.d.

be advanced as our marine Intercourse with the north will not open
[p. 2.] earlier, however from the variety of orders given to search for this
Book I should fondly hope to get at least one Copy of it.

Mr Low's Collections are now out of my hands, being consigned
to the revisal of his English Friends, who must determine the publication or rejection of the M.SS. of this will write you afterwards as
some time must elapse to engrave the drawings which are many should
it appear in publick.

Since I wrote you last, have been informed that a Clergyman [4] on
the Banks of *Galawater* which joins Tweed has been collecting the
old Ballads, Songs &c that either have been composed *by* natives or
by others on various Incidents which happened in Ettrick Forrest or
Selkirkshire and it's neighbourhood, if I can get any further accounts
of this Collection or if he will permit your revisal of it, a solicitation
shall take place by some acquaintance or other in his vicinity for this
latter purpose, in this a week or two may pass 'ere a proper person
may be found out to gain my desired end.

Your address is so distinct that it shall be observed in the way
directed, it will give me satisfaction to execute any of your requests
from this Country by

Revd Dear Sir

Your much obliged and obedient

humble Servt   GPaton

Customhouse Edinburgh
  6 September 1777

PS. Mr Gough has rendered Orkney respectable in Antiquity by his
accurate and curious Dissertation on the Treasure of Canute's Coins
found there anno 1774 under the Title of "Table of the Coins of
Canute King of England and Denmark" 4to 1777 [5] with an engraved plate of the Horn in which these were found and views of

---

[4] This clergyman cannot be identified with any certainty.
[5] *A Catalogue of the Coins of Ca-*
nute, King of Denmark and England,
1777.

Fibulae deposited near them: the variety amount to N° 42. of these he had sight of: others were hastily disperst on the discovery.
GP

Address: The Reverend Dr Thomas Percy
Easton Mauduit

Docket: Of Norne Poetry.

CIII

From Percy¹

Easton Mauduit, July 20.1778

Dear Sir,

Tho' a long Interval has elapsed since the Suspension of our Correspondence, I have been constantly wishing to renew it, and cannot delay any longer to make inquiries after your health: Which I hope has not suffered since I heard from you.—Of this I cannot but wish to be informed, as soon as you can find leisure: and also to know what literary Persuits have lately engaged your | Attention. Any Information on the preceding Subjects will ever be most acceptable to me.—In return, perhaps it may not be unsatisfactory to you to know that the Bristoll Poetry,² which for these 3 or 4 years past has so much engaged the Attention of the Critics at this End of the Island, is to demonstration proved to be modern,³ in an apendix lately published by the ingenious Editor of those Poems | (viz Thomas Tyrwhitt⁴ [p. 3.]

[p. 2.]

¹ *Source:* National Library of Scotland, MS. 29-5-8, Vol. I, f. 91; printed in Maidment, pp. 72–73.
² *Poems, Supposed To Have Been Written At Bristol, By Thomas Rowley, and Others . . . The Third Edition; To Which Is Added An Appendix,* 1778, 8°. See an account of the controversy in *A Life of Thomas Chatterton* by E. H. W. Meyerstein, 1930, pp. 449–99.
³ Over "spurious" deleted.
⁴ Thomas Tyrwhitt (1730–86), Fellow of Merton College, Oxford;

Esq late Clerk of the House of Commons) and what is most aston-
ishing, to have been written by a Youth, who died 2 months before he
was 18.—If the Volume of the said Poetry in 8ᵛᵒ and the said Apendix
fall in your way: they will much amuse you.

I hope you will believe me to be, with great Regard

Dear Sir

Your faithful

Servant

Thomas Percy

[p. 4.] PS/

May I intreat the favour of you to forward the inclosed as directed.
Any Letter may be forwarded to me under Cover

To

 The Earl of Sussex *P*

  at Easton Mauduit

  (By Bozeate Bag)

   Northamptonshire

Be careful to add the *P* for Distinction as I shall be much from
home all Summer; be pleased to attribute to absence any future
delay in acknowledging your obliging favours.

CIV

From Paton[1]

[August 4, 1778]

Dear Revᵈ Sir

It is many months since the problematical authenticity of *Rowley's Poems* did engage Parties here, soon after I fortunately obtain'd,
thro' the attention of a very worthy friend, a Copy of the Poems; it

---

Clerk to the House of Commons, editor of Chaucer's *Canterbury Tales*
and of Aristotle's *Poetics*.

[1] *Source:* British Museum, Add.
MS. 32332, ff. 118–19.

created an astonishment how so young a Man, as *Chatterton,* should execute such a Collection, which upon a repeated perusal of these various lines do appear, to me, to wear the intrinsic proofs of a *modern hand:* but how much must it be admired that this juvenile composer should have so remarkably palm'd his lines on the Public?—had not this been the Case; his Genius had great merit, or had the length of his days been prolonged to [have] obliged the world with riper compositions he might have truely deserved the uncontroverted esteem of poetical admirers—The Appendix | has not appeared here [p. 2.] yet that I can learn but have ordered it from the South: Accept of my best thanks for the Information of the accurate Publisher of these Poems, and discoverer of the Imposition.

The late unexpected great attention to Business, in our way, has much distracted my Notice in Literary way, but hope as the one subsides the other may prevail. I beg leave only to inform you that a few days ago, an Acquaintance designing for London one of these days took charge of a *Specimen* of a proposed work under the Title of *Bibliotheca Septentrionalis,* (which will be left at Northumberland house for you) by *M*ʳ *Callender of Craigforth:* [2] I'm apt to believe the Plan is not yet properly digested for public Communication, but am well assured besides what he may have already composed, he is very attentively | engaged in collecting all the materials seemingly [p. 3.] necessary and usefull to expedite the Scheme; which hope may be received with a generous, candid welcome from the World: if you have not already read the Specimen I humbly submit it to your friendly countenance.

It shall always give me sensible satisfaction to learn you are well and that you have relished the Sweets of good health these many months, long be it Your and Yours happy situation.

On the reception of your last favour the inclosed was safely conveyed as the address instructed, and must plead to be excused for

[2] John Callander of Craigforth (d. 1789). *Speedily will be published Bibliotheca Septentrionalis, or an Universal Dictionary containing everything relating to the Northern nations,* Bell and Murray, Edinburgh, 1778, folio, pp. 13. An interleaved copy of this "specimen" is in the British Museum, 803, m. 3. The work did not appear.

not giving you such assurances earlier, have not had it in my power before now to write you.

[p. 4.]   In a few Posts hence as the *favourable Covers* under the *Earl of Essex'* protection will permit, you may expect a sheet or two of some lines promised me by the Collector[3] of the Two Vol. of our *Scots Songs,* which he has pickt up (he tells me) thro' much application from the memory of some friend, believe it may be of the Historical kind; of which will say nothing till it reache you, when all other information given me shall be communicated.

I ever am

Dear Sir

Your most obedient and

obliged humble Servt

GPaton

Customh° Edinburgh

4 August 1778

CV

From Paton[1]

[September 10, 1778]

Rear Revd Sir

Having just now been favoured with the Fragment of a Ballad[2] mentioned in my last I beg leave to transmit the same as it came to my hand: another friend has promised me another which may be expected in a few Posts hence. I am affraid these will afford you small

---

[3] David Herd.

[1] *Source:* British Museum, Add. MS. 32332, f. 120.

[2] "The Duke he was a Bonny Lad," in a copyist's hand and entitled "Fragment of an Old Ballad. 1345"

(Add. MS. 32332, ff. 121–26). There are two copies of a longer version entitled "The Duke of Milk" in David Herd's MSS.: Add. MS. 22311, ff. 120–27 and Add. MS. 22312, ff. 3–10.

or no Amusement but as they are cannot restrain them from your perusal.

I should wish to know what composes the *Pepysian Collection* of M.SS.³ &ᶜ when this was begun and what these may consist of, or if wholy in the poetical strain? I am with all respect

Revᵈ Dear Sir
Your most obedᵗ Servᵗ
GPaton

Customh° Edinbʳ
10 Septʳ 1778

CVI
From Percy¹

Alnwick Castle, Septʳ 30.1778

Dear Sir,

I should not have let your obliging Favours remain so long un-acknowledged, but being forwarded to me in the South, it was some time before I could get them sent back to me here. I accept them very thankfully and consider them as most obliging Proofs of your kind attention. The Plan of the Bibliotheca Septentrionalis gives us to expect a curious Work which I wish the Author Health and spirits to accomplish: I remember Dʳ Johnson once told me he had intended in an early part of his Life to compose a Dictionary | of English [p. 2.] or British Antiquities: ²—Many articles in which must have suited this Plan of Mʳ Callander's, but I believe he never began it.

³ See Letter CVI, n. 3, p. 158.
¹ *Source:* National Library of Scotland, MS. 29-5-8, Vol. I, f. 92; printed in Maidment, pp. 73–75.
² The Dictionary of English or British Antiquities is not included in the catalogue of works that he had thought of: see Boswell's *Life* (ed. Hill and Powell, 1934), IV, 381–83.

I thank you for the Copy of the Scots Ballad, "The Duke he was a bonny Lad." I see it is dated 1345, but this I suppose is only to be understood of the Events recited: for as for the Composition it is certainly very modern.—

In the same Letter that inclosed "The Duke" you talk of sending me another Fragment, but it is not yet come to hand, which I only mention lest it should have miscarried thro' a Mistake in the Direction, as you talked of inclosing to me under Cover to the Earl of *Essex: Sussex* is the Name (excuse my reminding you of it, and always to be distinguished by a *P* or they miscarry)

[p. 3.]   You ask about the Pepysian Collection of MSS.—Mr. Pepys's Library which he bequeathed to Magdalene College in Cambridge, consists almost only of Printed Books, among which he has a large Collection of old English *Printed* Ballads, pasted in 5 large folio volumes of Blank Paper:—He has indeed one very curious Volume of Scots Ballads and Poems in MS. written by one of the Maitlands [3] of Lauderdale [4] about the Time of K. James 5th out of which I have transcribed a great Part of the Contents: Many of the Poems are copies of the same that are in Bannatyne's MS in your Advocates Library. I am very truly

> Dear Sir
> Your obliged & faithful Servant
> Thomas Percy

Address: To Mr Paton
at the Custom House
Edinburgh.

[3] The Maitland MS., bought by Samuel Pepys (1633–1703) at the Lauderdale sale in 1692 and bequeathed by him to Magdalene College Library, Cambridge.
[4] A mistake for Lethington.

CVII
From Paton[1]

[October 6, 1778]

Revd Dear Sir

Accept of gratefull acknowledgements for the kind communications about Mr Pepys Library, [in] which you corrected a mistake of my apprehending the Collection to have been deposited in London but appear to have been bequeathed by the original Possessor to the Cambridge University: the perusal of the M.S. Volume must have afforded you satisfaction and the more so that it contains *Maitland's Poems*. which are in Bannatyne's M.S. in the Advocates' Library, I do believe if these had been markt [2] in this Collection it would [have] been a most valuable acquisition to the Book, as these Poems by Maitland are not so frequent or well known in this Country now.

Your remarks on the Scots' Ballad as to the date and Composition of *"The Duke he was a bonny Lad"*, is very just. the date plainly referrs to the Time of the Event and the Lines very Modern.— The person who promised me the Fragment has been in the Country ever since my writing you last and this is the only reason why it has not been hitherto transmitted, how soon he returns and these put into my hands they shall be immediately transmitted either to Alnwick Castle or London as you may please to instruct me: it will be a few weeks hence 'ere the Gentleman appear in Town again.

I beg pardon for the inattention of the Address, which in future will be corrected.

[1] *Source:* British Museum, Add. MS. 32332, f. 127.
[2] In Pinkerton's "Account of the Contents of the Maitland and Bannatyne MSS." (*Ancient Scotish Poems*, 1786, II, Appendix) poems common to both MSS. are marked with an asterisk. (It was Percy who had called Pinkerton's attention to the Maitland MS.: see Nichols's *Illustrations*, VIII, 113.) See also *The Bannatyne Manuscript*, ed. Ritchie, I, cx–cxx.

Mr Callander, I believe, is very attentively engaged in the composition and arrangement of his *"Bibliotheca Septentrionalis"* for which purpose has been for several years and is daylie collecting from foreign parts Books to expedite his designed Work, which is a very extensive Plan, requiring a very general Correspondence and assist-
[p. 2.] ance from every one whose study has | been employed in that line of Literature, and do suppose he must cordialy welcome every generous communications in this branch of Knowledge: if Dr Johnson turned his thoughts this Way, what ever collections he had made on that department would (am apt to believe) be very acceptable to Mr Callander in furthering this work, which does seem to take in a most extensive field, comprehending discoveries of the more remote and darker Periods of former Days.

If not much mistaken, I think, sometime ago You gave me a hint of your publishing a *fourth Volume* to the *Reliques of ancient Poetry*. Have you any thoughts of obliging the World this way? and how soon may this happen?

The high Encomiums bestowed on our Scot's Poets by Mr Warton,[3] (whose Work have only glanced at) has raised a kind of scheme to publish (if it should meet with proper Encouragement) *Andro Winton's Chronicle of Scotland,*[4] which may be succeeded by some other Works of latter times: but this is only yet thought of no proposals or concert having been as yet made, the new Edition of Chaucer [5] with the Glossary, as yet unknown here, will be of great Service, with your valueable Glossaries, in any Publications of this sort. I ever am

Revd Dear Sir

Your most obedient and much obliged

humble Servt GPaton

[3] *The History of English Poetry,* 1778, II, 257–335. There are three sections, giving Warton a claim to be the first historian of Scottish poetry.

[4] *De Orygynale Cronykil of Scotland, be Androw of Wyntown, Priowr of Sanct Serfis Ynche in Loch Levyn.*

Now first published, with Notes, a Glossary, etc. by David Macpherson. London: Printed by T. Bensley. M.DCC.XCV., 8°, 2 vols.

[5] *The Canterbury Tales,* edited by Thomas Tyrwhitt (1730–86), 1775. The glossary appeared in 1778.

Customhouse Edinburgh
  6 October 1778

Address: The Reverend Dr Thomas Percy
    Alnwick Castle

Docket: Mr Paton

CVIII
From Percy[1]

Carlisle (the Deanery) Novr 27th 1778.

Dear Sir,

I flatter myself you will excuse my long delay in acknowledging your last obliging Favour, in Consideration of the multiplicity of Business and variety of avocations, in which my late preferment[2] has involved me, and which for some time to come, I fear, will leave me no leisure for those agreeable literary amusements, which have been the Subject of your many obliging Letters. Tho' I am only come down here for a few days,[3] and shall return Southward almost immediately, I could not allow myself to leave this place, without first paying my respects to you on paper, and touching on some of the Points, you mention, in your last Letter.

With respect to Mr Callander's very extensive Work, I can only [p. 2.] contribute my good Wishes, that it may be brought to the requisite Perfection, as my present Situation will I fear afford me no leisure for resuming those amusing Disquisitions and Researches, which some years ago, I persued with great Pleasure. As for Dr Johnson, I

---

[1] *Source:* National Library of Scotland, MS. 29-5-8, Vol. I, f. 93; printed in Maidment, pp. 75–77.

[2] Percy had become Dean of Carlisle in the autumn of 1778.

[3] Percy arrived at Carlisle 20 November and departed for Easton Mauduit 6 December (see his *Journal*).

do not believe he could afford much assistance now for a Work of that kind, as his Time has been otherwise employed for many years. With regard to the Reliques of Antient Poetry, I have a large fund of Materials which when my Son [4] has compleated his Studies at the University, he may if he likes it, distribute into one or more [p. 3.] additional Volumes: but I myself shall | hardly find a Vacancy now from more serious persuits, to carry them forward myself. I find not quite the same relish for those little amusing literary sallies, as I did 15 or 16 years ago when the former Volumes were digested. However. I still find remaining so much of my wonted Liking for these old pieces, that they may afford me still a Relaxation from graver Studies and you will always much oblige me therefore by communicating any thing of that sort which may occur to you. As my residence with the Duke of Northumberland will now cease, it will not be advisable for the future to inclose any thing for me under Cover to his Grace; but send it to Easton Mauduit under the Directions to the Earl of Sussex (with a *P* for distinction as usual). I remain

Dear Sir

Your most obedient Servant

Thomas Percy

PS/

I am glad to hear that there is an Intention of publishing *Andro Winton's Chronicle of Scotland,* and other Pieces of that Sort: I wish they were seriously begun and regularly persued in a Series without Interruption till all your old MSS were published.

Address: To Mr Paton
at the Custom House
Edinburgh

---

[4] Henry Percy (b. 1763) died at Marseilles 1783. There was no additional volume. A fourth edition, under the nominal editorship of Percy's nephew, Thomas Percy (1768–1808), fellow of St. John's College, Oxford, was published in 1794.

CIX
From Paton[1]

[December 4, 1778]

Revd Dear Sir

From the place of Residence of your late Preferment your most agreeable Favours came last day to hand. Accept of my best Salutations on this, believe me I desire your advancement in the Church &^c may be ever to your Wish, and altho' less time may be spared for the innocent relaxations in the Literary pursuits, which have so happily employed a vacant Hour for some Years past, yet amidst these additional cares and attentions to the superior and more interesting concerns of Mankind it's to be hoped you may find a few moments occasionaly to renew these former researches, which will continualy give pleasure to the Publick.

Your Sentiments with respect to Mr Callender's Work I shall take care to have conveyed him (for I have no personal acquaintance of the Gentleman) make no doubt of his ready acceptance in what your convenient time may spare to communicate. Dr Johnson's political attachments[2] of late Years must unquestionably attract all his thoughts in that Line so no assistance can be expected from that Quarter.

Give me leave to congratulate you on the promising hopes and happy views you enjoy in Your Son's application to Letters, who shall merit the publick regard afterwards both from his own but your justly esteem'd abilities: heartily do I rejoice in his advancing pursuits, these materials must prove a treasure of future amusements, which we may sometime hence be equaly pleased to see.

---

[1] *Source:* Harvard College Library, bMS Eng 893 (124G).
[2] Johnson's political activity ceased with the publication of *Political* *Tracts*, 1776. In December 1778 he was engaged on the *Prefaces, Biographical and Critical*, which became *The Lives of the Poets.*

As it is (most incorrectly written &^c) please receive these few lines on *"Gillnockie"* ³ and *"Lord Maxwell's last good night."* ⁴ What else may come into my possession shall be forwarded as occasion may invite.

Hitherto no regular Plan has been concerted about the Publication [p. 2.] of *Andro Winton's Chronicle*, or any of our other | Scots' Poets, the general distresses of the Times as also the unhappy situation of this Country occasioned by a misfortunate Banking Company do great injury to us and even have crampt every literary Project, it's to be hoped in some years hence that Storm may blow over.

I shall ever regard the instructions of addressing you and omit giving His Grace of Northumberland any trouble being ever

Revd Dear Sir

Your most obedient and obliged
humble Servant   GPaton

Customhouse Edinburgh
4 December 1778

Address: The Reverend Dr Thomas Percy
Easton Mauduit

CX

From Percy¹

Northumb^d House Jan.2.1779

Dear Sir

I received your last obliging favour which like all your former, demands my best acknowledgments for the very kind attention ex-

---

³ "Johnie Armstrong," first published by Allan Ramsay in *The Ever Green*, 1724.

⁴ The version sent by Paton to Percy is printed in Child's *English and Scottish Popular Ballads*, VII (No. 195), p. 34. The ballad first appeared in a variant version from the Glenriddell MS. in *The Minstrelsy of the Scottish Border*, 1802, I, 194.

¹ *Source:* National Library of Scotland, MS. 29-5-8, Vol. I, f. 94; printed in Maidment, p. 78.

pressed in it. I only desire to set right one particular; I wished in my former Letter to be understood, as apologizing for the little assistance, which it would now be in my power to afford to such curious and ingenious Disquisitions as Mr Calander's, in short wishing to have it properly represented that I should now have no leisure at all to promote those amusing Researches by any | Contributions [p. 2.] and you seem to have taken my meaning just contrary as implying a promised assistance. I know not whether it is worth while to say any more about it, but I could not refrain from setting the matter in a true light to you; as I should be sorry to be thought to enter into Engagements, which it is impossible for me to perform. I wish you many happy New Years and remain

Dear Sir
Your obliged Servant.
Tho:Percy

PS/
I am returning to Easton Mauduit.

Address: To Mr Paton
at the Custom-house
Edinburgh.

APPENDIX I

Letters Illustrating the Correspondence of Percy and Paton

I

From Paton to Robert Lambe [1]

[March 21, 1768].

Reverend Sir [2]

I would have answered Your Favours of 29ᵗʰ past sooner, had I been at Home when it reached this Place.

When Mʳ Murray [3] was in Town I shewed him a very old *Collection of Scots Poems printed by Andro Hart* [4] about the Year 1600 or older, but am at a great Loss to know what kind of Poems Mʳ Percy wants, so you will please be so good as tender him My Compliments and express my fondness of being informed from himself, what he is most earnest to be possessed of, assuring him that he shall have the Use of any that are my Property or what I collect for him: This Collection above mentioned is said to be written by *King James the first,* [5] which Book I presume Mʳ Percy never saw at least another Copy of it is not to be met in any Liberary here.

It will be kind if Mʳ Percy intimates, what Collections of Scots Poems he has already seen, whereby I may be assured to acquaint him, what may be procured for him, he ought particularly to take notice of the Subjects on which these Poems are composed, that he wants.

[1] *Source:* British Museum, Add. MS. 32332, f. 11.
[2] See Letter I, n. 2, p. 1.
[3] John Murray the first, bookseller (d. 6 November 1793).
[4] See Letter I, n. 18, p. 3.
[5] See Letter III, p. 8.

167

Believe me how soon I receive your or Mr Percy's Answer that a
Reply shall be made immediately and am

Revd Sir
Your most obedient humble
Servant
GPaton

Customhouse Edinburgh
21st March 1768

Address: To The Revd Mr Lambe
at Norham
near Berwick

II

From John Wotherspoon to Paton [1]

[August 29, 1774]

Sir

My friend Mr Herd obliged me with a sight of Dr Percy's letter [2]
to you respecting the Scottish Songs &c. which I now return.—Be
pleased to inform that gentleman, that we chearfully consent to his
making the use he proposes of our M.S. vol. by extracting such fragments as he thinks proper to adopt into his plan. These mutilated
antiques thus perfected and restored by Dr Percy, will give us a
pleasure resembling that which we should feel from beholding the
injuries of time on a statue of Phidias of Polycletus repaired by the
hand of Buonarruoti.[3] With equal frankness we will accept the
offer the D^r is so good as to make us of extracts from Maitland's M.S.
and would be obliged to him for pointing out what he most approves
in Banatyne's. We would be happy to receive and to follow any

---

[1] *Source:* British Museum, Add.
MS. 32332, ff. 77–78. For Wotherspoon, see Letter LXIX, n. 2, p. 103.

[2] See Letter LXVIII, p. 101.
[3] Michelangelo Buonarroti (1475–
1564).

hints which Dr Percy would suggest for the improvement of our plan, and proud of the liberty to acknowledge in our preface the honour of his assistance.

The publication of our 2^d vol. will necessarily be delayed for some [p. 2.] time. The first being out of print, we propose to begin by reprinting that, with more perfect versions of some of the songs, expunging some of the most imperfect fragments, revising the orthography throughout, and annexing a glossary; [4] in the meantime the 2^d vol. will be preparing for the press, in the same manner.

We are grateful to Dr Percy for his permission to avail ourselves of his intended addition to the Reliques, in case we should think of publishing a 3° vol. of Scots Songs; and we are particularly obliged to you for the trouble you have taken in this matter.

I am

Sir

Your most h^{ble} Servt

J. Wotherspoon

Edin^r 29 Aug. 1774

P.S. I enclose a paragraph of an Essay on the Theatre intended to [p. 3.] be prefixed to a collection of Plays [5] now printing in this town, in which as I presume to differ from a sentiment of Dr Percy's, in his short, but elegant Essay on the English Stage, you may, if you think proper, transmit it to him, and desire him to return it.—Had I the honour of his acquaintance, I should personally acknowledge my obligations for the light I derived from his Essay on this subject.

*Address:*To Mr. George Paton
Of the Customhouse
Edin^r

---

[4] See Letter XI, n. 4, p. 20.
[5] *The Theatre, Tragic and Comic. With an introductory Essay on the origin and progress of the English* *stage,* Edinburgh, 1776, 14 vols., 12°. It is included in the Book List in the *Scots Magazine,* July, 1776, p. 383.

III

From John Wotherspoon to Percy [1]

[July 27, 1775]

Revd Sir

It is now a twelvemonth since the M. S. vol. of Scots Songs were put into your hands by Mr Paton, and so long has their publication been postponed on that account. As it is intended to publish both volumes forthwith, it will be obliging to return the M.S. vol. either to me or to Mr Paton.[2] If Dr Percy has completed any of the fragments in the manner he proposed,[3] we should be happy to insert with his leave, these supplements in our publication; and we beg leave respectfully to remind him of the promise he was so good as make us with regard to Sir Richd Maitland's M.S. Songs &c. And any hints or directions the D^r may be pleased to communicate with respect to this publication will be received with grateful deference, by

Revd Sir
Your most h^{ble} Servt
J. Wotherspoon

Edin^r 27 July 1775

P.S. A letter or parcel directed to me printer here, will come safe:— otherwise it may come thro' the hands of Mr Paton.

[1] *Source:* British Museum, Add. MS. 32332, f. 96.
[2] See Letter LXXXII, p. 120.
[3] See Letter LXVIII, p. 101.

APPENDIX II

David Herd's *Ancient and Modern Scottish Songs*, 1776

The Percy-Paton correspondence throws light on the second edition of David Herd's *Ancient and Modern Scottish Songs*, published in two volumes, 1776, and on the part played in it by Percy.

Percy had seen the first edition in one volume shortly after it came out in 1769, and he made suggestions for improvements in any future edition.[1] These Paton passed on to the publisher, John Wotherspoon, with the result that Percy, whose interest was only general to begin with, found himself by degrees committed to giving help.[2]

It has been argued[3] that Percy requested the publisher to show him the manuscript of the collection which was intended for the second edition; that as an inducement, he held out the hope of help and improvements; that when the manuscript was sent to him, he kept it for two years, then returned it abruptly without fulfilling any of his promises.

But the facts are very different. The first move was made not by Percy but by the collector and publisher, who approached him through Paton. This is placed beyond doubt by a letter from Paton of 17 October, 1772:[4] "I am desired by the Collector and Publisher of *the Collection of Scots Songs* . . . that he has now got together such a number as will make up another Volume, but the Share of Business that he is engaged in will not admit of the Care of publishing it, so requested me to write you if you would do it. . . ."

Percy immediately replied, "I will see what can be done."[5] The

[1] See Letter XI, p. 20.
[2] See Letter XXXIII, p. 44.
[3] Hecht, *Songs from David Herd's Manuscripts*, pp. 27–28.
[4] See Letter XXXII (preserved at Harvard), p. 41. Hecht cannot have

seen it, and he was not disposed to give Percy the benefit of the doubt.
[5] Hecht took Letter XXXIII (of 27 October) to be an approach by Percy. It was his reply to a request.

manuscript, however, was not sent to Percy till August 1774. When at last enabled to inspect it, he found that most of the pieces were "Fragments too mutilated and imperfect to afford much pleasure to a reader in their present State," and he went on to make some practical proposals. He felt he could restore some of the fragments but, to avoid delay, suggested that the editor should proceed to compile his second volume from pieces that were "tolerably perfect," and he offered to help him with "a good number of old Scots Songs and Poems" that he had transcribed from the Maitland Manuscript at Cambridge. He also suggested that the editor might include suitable pieces from the Bannatyne Manuscript. The residue of the collection, with the fragments to be restored, should, he thought, be held in reserve for a third volume, and as he had a fourth volume of the *Reliques* in view, he proposed that there should be a free exchange of material for these two projects.[6]

Percy's suggestions were readily accepted. But there were delays and further changes of plan. Percy was becoming more and more burdened with other work, and in the end, he had to send the manuscript back without making any use of its contents. But he did not consider that this canceled the earlier agreement. He was still ready to keep his side of it and to send some poems from the Maitland Manuscript.[7] Before this was done, the *Songs* appeared in two volumes in 1776, a few days previous to the death of the publisher.

---

[6] See Letter LXVIII (22 August 1774), p. 101.

[7] See Letter LXXXIII (28 July 1775), p. 122.

APPENDIX III
The Bannatyne Manuscript

The composition of the Bannatyne Manuscript has confronted editors with some difficulties. These chiefly concern a section of fifty-eight pages beginning "Heir begynnis ane ballat buik written In the zeir of god 1568" and ending with "The song of the rid square." The editor [1] of the first complete edition of the Bannatyne Manuscript, printed for the Hunterian Club of Glasgow in four volumes (1873–1901), concluded that these pages were not part of the manuscript proper and placed them at the end. The editor of the Scottish Text Society's edition in four volumes (Edinburgh, 1928–34) placed them at the beginning of Volume I but, noting that most of the poems appeared again in the manuscript in a different order and with variations in the text, suggested that this section might be a draft or duplicate manuscript representing "Bannatyne's first attempt in the way of an anthology." [2]

What has, till now, rested on conjecture is put beyond doubt by the discovery of the following letter from the Earl of Hyndford to Percy.[3]

Prestongrange [4] Janr: 6. 1773

Sir

This serves to acknowledge your esteem'd favours of the 26th past and to testify how unworthy I think my self of the compliments you pay me. I hope the manuscript [5] will come safe to your hand

---

[1] James Barclay Murdoch.
[2] Vol. I, xv. This view had been put forward by J. T. T. Brown in the *Scottish Historical Review*, Glasgow, 1904, Vol. I, p. 138.
[3] Presented to the National Library

of Scotland by Professor D. Nichol Smith, 24 March 1943. MS. 3109, ff. 72–73.
[4] Near Haddington, East Lothian.
[5] See Letter XXXVI, p. 52.

and upon the subject of it I think it necessary to inform you that I gave two M.S.S. to the Advocates library which I understand they have now bound up together,[6] the largest was wrote out by Bannantine,[7] as the first page bears, and concludes with a remuneratory poem of Allan Ramsays to my father for the use of it in compiling his Evergreen, the other which is but about a fourth part of the size of Bannantine's performance has no connection with it, appears to be much more used, and have not title to be bound up together but as they both came from the hand of your humble servant. I thought proper to acquaint you of this circumstance that no more be ascribed to Bannantine than is due—I hope you will excuse this trouble and believe I remain with great regard and esteem—

Sir

Your most obedient

humble Servant

Hyndford

The later history of the Bannatyne Manuscript thus becomes clear. Hyndford gave two manuscripts to the Advocates' Library in 1772, one being the Bannatyne and the other, as Hyndford states, having "no connection with it." [8] But the Curators had them bound together, and this composite manuscript came to be known as the Bannatyne Manuscript. In the nineteenth century, it was decided that the Manuscript should be inlaid and rebound. The Minutes of the Curators and of the Faculty of Advocates do not indicate when this was done, but from the binding, a date about 1825 can be assumed. Had the composite nature of the Manuscript been realized, the shorter might have been kept separate from the Bannatyne. But instead of this, the composite manuscript was divided into two more or less equal parts and bound in two volumes with the titles "Bannatyne's Manuscript Vol. I" and "Bannatyne's Manuscript Vol. II." This has resulted in an awkward and misleading division, for Volume

---

[6] See Appendix IV, "Curators' Minutes."

[7] Not uncommon as a variant.

[8] The two manuscripts, however, appear to be in the same hand.

I consists of the shorter manuscript and the first 163 folios of the Bannatyne Manuscript proper, and Volume II contains the rest of the Bannatyne Manuscript, including the "table of the haill Buik," which applies only to the contents of the Bannatyne and not to the short manuscript.

The composite nature of the Manuscript in its present form can be further seen from the two methods of numbering employed. Throughout volumes I and II, the pages are numbered consecutively in pencil; but on page 61, which is "the first leif" of the Bannatyne Manuscript proper, folio numbering begins, and the references in the "table of the haill Buik" are to folios.

It seems that when they were separate, the short manuscript was numbered in pages and the Bannatyne in folios. After they had been bound together, pagination was made continuous. At what date this took place is not known, but Percy, in his annotated copy of Lord Hailes's *Ancient Scottish Poems* (1770), which he had collated with the Bannatyne Manuscript between 1773–75, gives page references to poems in the short manuscript but uses the folio numbering for those in the Manuscript itself.[9] An example may be taken from his note on "The Prais of Ege," page 108, which reads: "Collated loosely with two Copies in Banatyne's MS. The one is fo. 57. marked B. the other at the beginning in pag. 32. mark^d B.2."

The following may be noted:

Allan Ramsay's transcript of Lindsay's "Satire of the Three Estates," with marginal notes by Percy.[10]

Percy's annotated copy of the *Ever Green* (1761), National Library of Scotland, MS. 494–95.

Hailes's interleaved copy of the *Ever Green* (1761), now in the possession of Cleanth Brooks, Yale University.

---

[9] The penciled pagination runs on mechanically without indicating gaps in the foliation where leaves are missing. An error occurs where folio 58a is paged 175 and folio 58b is misnumbered 178 for 176.

The foliation in the Manuscript and in the "table of the haill Buik" is in Arabic numerals, but Roman figures are decipherable on more than 150 leaves. These do not seem to have any special significance for the history of the arrangement of the Manuscript.

[10] See Letter LXVI, n. 3, p. 99.

Percy's annotated copy of Hailes's *Ancient Scottish Poems* (1770), National Library of Scotland (Press-mark Ry. IV. f. 4).

The Borrowing of the Bannatyne Manuscript

Percy first mentioned his "extravagant Wish" to borrow the Bannatyne Manuscript in a letter to Lord Hailes,[11] and it was at the request of John, fourth Earl of Hyndford, who had given the Manuscript to the Advocates' Library in 1772, that the Curators agreed to let it out of their keeping.[12] The correspondence with Paton gives a full account of this transaction, for Paton was entrusted with packing and dispatching the Manuscript and was associated, as his letters show, with efforts to have the time allowed to Percy extended. It was to Paton that the Manuscript was returned, to be deposited again in the Advocates' Library after being in Percy's hands for over two years.

Percy made considerable use of the Bannatyne Manuscript. He copied poems for his intended anthologies. He collated versions of poems found also in the Maitland Manuscript; he collated Lord Hailes's edition of *Ancient Scottish Poems* (1770) with the originals in the Bannatyne Manuscript.[13] He collated, sometimes cursorily, sometimes minutely, various poems in the 1761 edition of the *Ever Green*,[14] and he collated in part a transcript of Lindsay's "Satire of the Three Estates" made from the Bannatyne Manuscript by Allan Ramsay.[15] In the Manuscript itself, Percy made at least 105 additions to the "table of the haill Buik." He emended the third line of the last stanza of "The song of the rid square"; he added catch words at the end of folios 299b and 301b, and titles to several of the Fables between folios 299a and 345a.[16]

[11] Percy-Hailes *Correspondence*, p. 121.
[12] See Appendix IV, "Curators' Minutes," p. 179.
[13] Percy-Hailes *Correspondence*, Appendix II, p. 161.
[14] Copy preserved in the National Library of Scotland, MS. 494–95.
[15] See Letter LV, p. 82, and Scottish Text Society's edition, I, xxiii–xxvi.
[16] Details are given in the Scottish Text Society's edition, I, xxvii.

It was suggested by David Laing [17] that the title in black ink and in a late hand on folio 1a is Percy's addition:

"Ane most Godlie, mirrie and lustie Rapsodie maide be sundrie learned Scots poets and written be George Bannatyne in the tyme of his youth."

It is not in Percy's usual hand, but it does resemble closely an italic script that he often employed when collating.

[17] See an article by J. T. T. Brown   Glasgow, 1904, I, 139. in the *Scottish Historical Review,*

APPENDIX IV
Extracts from Minutes: The Advocates' Library

*Minutes of the Curators of the
Advocates' Library*

Advocates Library 14 Feb. 1772.

"Mr Robert Cullen produced a Letter from the Right Honourable
the Earl of Hyndford addressed to the Curators for the Advocates
Library; the Tenor of which follows

St. Johns Street Febr. 10th 1772

To the Curators of the Advocates Library

This antient collection of Scots Poems, which does so much honour
to our Country, and to the Age in which the[y] were composed,
is presented to the Advocates Library, as the most worthy reposi-
tory for so rare a performance by their most Obedient and most
humble Servant (sic Subscrib.) Hyndford.

Ordered that the aforesaid valuable Manuscript be placed in
the Advocates Library and that the name of the noble Donor be
insert in the Register of Donations."

19th June 1772
"Ordered that the Librarian make a Scroll of a letter of thanks to
the Earl of Hyndford for his valuable present of a MS. collection of
antient Scottish Poems to be laid before the Curators at next meeting."

17th November 1772
"There was laid before the Curators a letter from Mr John Davidson of 16th October last upon the part of Mr Thomas Percy desiring
that the Curators would lend to him the Two manuscript volumes of
poems lately presented to the Library by the Earl of Hyndford together with a letter from the Earl of Hyndford 10th October last

mentioning that had these manuscripts remained with him Mr Percy should have free access to them and expressing his inclination that he should have the same Indulgence from the Faculty. The Curators are of opinion that they should lay this matter before the Faculty before giving any answer to Mr Davidson and in the mean time a letter should be wrote to Lord Hyndford to know whether his Lordship wished that the manuscript should be sent to Mr Percy out of the Library or that he should only have access to them in the Library: recommended to Mr Cullen to write the above Letter to the Earl of Hyndford."

8th December 1772
"The Curators having considered the Minute of Faculty of the fifth instant are of opinion that the two volumes of manuscript poems now bound in one volume may be lent to Mr Percy upon a Receipt from Mr John Davidson writer to the Signet binding himself to return the same to the Library at the end of six months after the date of the Receipt under the Penalty of fifty pounds sterling besides performance which Receipt shall also mention the conditions of the loan expressed in the Faculty's minute whereof a copy may be given to Mr Davidson to be transmitted to Mr Percy."

Minutes of the Faculty of Advocates, 1751–83

pp. 347–48   Edin^r 5th Decemb^r 1772
"Mr John Swinton Junr represented that there was laid before him and the other Curators a letter from Mr John Davidson writer to the Signet (dated 16th October last) upon the part of Mr Thomas Percy author of the reliques of ancient Poetry desiring that the Curators would lend to him the two manuscript volumes of Poems lately presented to the Library by the Earl of Hyndford together with a letter from the said Earl expressing his wish that Mr Percys desire should be complied with; Mr Swinton further represented that the Curators at their last meeting resolved to lay this affair before the Faculty for their direction: The Dean and Faculty having heard and considered this representation together with a letter from Lord

Hyndford the Donor are of opinion that Mr Percy should have a loan of the above manuscripts upon this condition that he shall not print the whole nor any part thereof without laying before the Curators a copy of such of them as he intends to print."

p. 350   12th Decemb^r 1772
"Upon reading the minute of the former meeting Mr John Swinton Junr moved that that clause respecting Mr Percys not being allowed to print any of the Poems contained in the M.S. lately presented to the Library by the Earl of Hyndford untill he should first lay before the Curators a copy of such of them as he may chuse to print, should be left out; The Dean and Faculty having heard Mr Swintons motion are of opinion that the minute cannot be altered as it contains a just representation of the then *Res gesta;* But that the Faculty at their next meeting would consider whether it was proper to alter that part of their resolution or not."

p. 351   Edin. 19th Decem^r 1772
"The Dean and Faculty having considered the motion which Mr John Swinton Junr made at last meeting do agree that that Clause of the minute of Faculty respecting Mr Percys being obliged to lay before the Curators a copy of such of Bannatines manuscript Poems as he may choose to print, be left out of the copy of the minute to be sent to Mr Percy."

Minutes of the Curators

[n.f.]   22^d Decem^r
"The Curators having taken under consideration that part of the last faculty minute allowing Bannatynes manuscript poems to be lent Mr Percy without obliging him to send down to the Curators a copy of what he intended to print direct that that condition be left out in the copy of the above mentioned minute to be sent him."

7th Janry 1773
"The Librarian having reported to the Curators that he had found great inconvenience attending the lending out of manuscripts which

were liable to be spoiled and often to be lost the Curators recall the regulation of 16th March, 1763 concerning the lending out of manuscripts and order that no manuscript whatever shall be lent out without an order of the Faculty."

Index